THE BOOK

This profound and eloquent meditation on
survival focuses on the concentration camps
under Hitler and Stalin—not to
document the horrors of torture and death,
but to illuminate the miraculous survival instinct.

THE AUTHOR

Born in Illinois in 1939, Terrence Des Pres
has been honored by both the
American Academy and Institute for Arts and
Letters (for distinction in literature, 1978)
and the National Jewish Book Awards
(Leon Jolson Award for a book on
the holocaust, 1978).

THE ACCLAIM

Of this *New York Times Book Review*
"Editors' Choice," *The Washington Post* has
written, "This is a horrifying, well-written,
moving account of how men and
women come to survive in the
worst of all possible worlds."

TERRENCE DES PRES

THE SURVIVOR

An Anatomy of Life in the Death Camps

WASHINGTON SQUARE PRESS
PUBLISHED BY POCKET BOOKS NEW YORK

Lines from "The Waste Land," in *Collected Poems 1909-1962*
by T. S. Eliot, copyright 1936 by Harcourt Brace Jovanovich,
Inc.; copyright © 1963, 1964 by T. S. Eliot; are reprinted by
permission of Harcourt Brace Jovanovich and Faber & Faber.

Portions of this book have been previously published elsewhere:
Chapter I in *Encounter* (September 1971); Chapter II in
Social Research (Winter 1973); and part of Chapter V in
Dissent (Winter 1976)

A Washington Square Press Publication of
POCKET BOOKS, a division of Simon & Schuster, Inc.
1230 Avenue of the Americas, New York, N.Y. 10020

Copyright © 1976 by Oxford University Press, Inc.

Published by arrangement with Oxford University Press,
New York
Library of Congress Catalog Card Number: 75-25468

ISBN: 0-671-46687-9

First Pocket Books printing March, 1977

10 9 8 7 6 5 4

WASHINGTON SQUARE PRESS, WSP and colophon are
registered trademarks of Simon & Schuster, Inc.

Printed in the U.S.A.

PREFACE

My subject is survival, the capacity of men and women to live beneath the pressure of protracted crisis, to sustain terrible damage in mind and body and yet be there, sane, alive, still human. I am not directly concerned with the concentration camps, but with the people who suffered those places, who endured that evil and returned to bear witness. Even so, an experience such as theirs cannot be understood apart from its context, and in the following pages there is much description, amounting almost to a comprehensive view, of camp conditions. Unavoidably, a spectacle of death and mutilation opens upon us, an endless silent scream rising to a sky forever heedless of men's anguish. But what mattered most for survivors—and what matters now for us—is a different aspect of the camp ordeal. Their testimony reveals a world ruled by death, but also a world of actual living conditions, of *ways of life* which are the basis and achievement of life in extremity. It turns out that survival is an experience with a definite structure, neither random nor regressive nor amoral. The aim of this book has been to make that structure visible.

And how does one handle this subject? One doesn't; not well, not finally. No degree of scope or care can equal the enormity of such events or suffice for the sorrow they encompass. Not to betray it is as much as I can hope for. The work itself took nearly four years, years of reading through vast amounts of eyewitness testimony, of cutting through accepted notions of the camp experience, of informal talk with survivors, and finally, before getting firmly underway, a time of search for a way to set myself in relation to them.

I could not take a stance of detachment, could not be "clinical" or "objective" in the way now thought proper. A curious fact about language, which Tolstoy and then Hemingway used to advantage, is that to write about terrible things in a neutral tone or with descriptions barren of subjective response tends to generate an irony so virulent as to end in either cynicism or despair. On the other hand, to allow feeling much play when speaking of atrocity is to border on hysteria and reduce the agony of millions to a moment of self-indulgence. There seemed one language left—a kind of archaic, quasi-religious vocabulary, which I have used not as a reflection of religious sentiment, but in the sense that only language of ultimate concern can be adequate to facts such as these.

As for point of view, I gradually came to see that I would have to stay within the survivor's own perspective. This will perhaps bother the historian, with his distrust of personal evidence; but radical suffering transcends relativity, and when one survivor's account of an event or circumstance is repeated in exactly the same way by dozens of other survivors, men and women in different camps, from different nations and cultures, then one comes to trust the validity of such reports and even to question rare departures from the general view. I had little choice, therefore, but to proceed by a dense use of quotation, by constant reference to examples and stories bearing the survivor's immediate authority. The book thus becomes a compilation of actual testimony—

the voices of many men and women gathered to a critical mass of rage and sorrow and truth. My job has been to provide a medium through which these scattered voices might issue in one statement.

The survivor is the figure who emerges from all those who fought for life in the concentration camps, and the most significant fact about their struggle is that it depended on fixed activities: on forms of social bonding and interchange, on collective resistance, on keeping dignity and moral sense active. That such thoroughly *human* kinds of behavior were typical in places like Buchenwald and Auschwitz amounts to a revelation reaching to the foundation of what man is. Facts such as these discredit the claims of nihilism and suggest, further, that when men and women must face months and years of death-threat they endure less through cultural than through biological imperatives. The biological sciences have begun to point in the same direction, and toward the end of the book I have incorporated some of their broader insights to clarify what survivors mean when they speak of *a talent for life,* or of life as a *power,* or of their reliance on *life in itself.* But here the reader should not be misled: speculation about the relation between survival behavior and basic life-processes is speculation only. The experience itself is what counts. An agony so massive should not be, indeed cannot be, reduced to a bit of datum in a theory.

In the concentration camps, as everyone knows, vastly more people died than came through. Statisticians may therefore wish to quarrel with my concern for the survivors. Fernand Braudel, a historian I greatly admire, argues that human destiny is shaped by sheer weight of numbers. Perhaps so, but that is not the issue here. We must not, in any case, confuse history with the constituent activities of selfhood. The image of the survivor includes any man or woman striving to keep life and spirit intact—not only those who returned, but the hundreds of thousands who stayed alive sometimes for years, only to die at the last minute. Nor do I think that numbers are as significant as the fact that survival behavior reveals typical forms of response to extremity.

I have tried to keep a wide range of reference, and to draw on descriptions from as much of the camp world as possible. For reasons which will be apparent, documentation of the Nazi experience is more extensive than that of its Soviet counterpart. And although the survivor is anyone from any corner of Europe or the Soviet Union (and often far beyond), this book is very much about the fate of the Jews, who fared worst in both German and Russian camps. But finally it is with ordinary people that I am concerned; with how they felt and what they did. At moments, the possibility that in some of the camps not one man or woman survived has caused a sense of futility strong enough to make going on seem pointless. Did anyone come back from Chelmno? Yet if no more than a dozen men and women stayed human and came through, if only the barest trace of humanness was *there* in the whole of that world, the survivor's experience would still be invaluable. And as Albert Camus put it, "human evidence must be preserved."

Hamilton, New York   T.D.P.
May 1975

ACKNOWLEDGMENTS

I began this book while a Junior Fellow at Harvard, and to the Society of Fellows, especially to Wassily Leontief and Reuben Brower, I owe an endless debt. I also owe special thanks to Alan Heimert, Master of Eliot House, who saw to it that I had a place to live and work unbothered. The book was completed while teaching at Colgate University, and for the kind support of my colleagues, Robert Blackmore in particular, I am most grateful. I received aid and encouragement from many people—friends, scholars, and not least the survivors I have come to know personally. At critical moments, assistance came from Lionel and Diana Trilling, E. O. Wilson, Patricia Blake, Liz Kornblee, Frederick Busch and James Raimes. Most of all I thank Stephanie Golden and Anthea Waleson.

CONTENTS

THE SURVIVOR

THE SURVIVOR IN FICTION

The writer's role is not free of difficult duties. By definition he cannot put himself today in the service of those who make history; he is at the service of those who suffer it.

ALBERT CAMUS

EACH THING, said Spinoza in the "Ethics," *insofar as it is in itself, endeavors to persevere in its being.* That may not be true for rocks and stars, but for societies and men it is undeniable. Survival of the body and its well-being take priority over everything else, although this imperative is transcended and lost sight of when the machinery of civilization is working as it should. The remarkable fact, however, is that while the business of living goes forward from day to day we reserve our reverence and highest praise for action which culminates in death. I am referring to images of the hero in Western religion and literature, and here there is no doubt: our serious models draw their sanction and compelling force from death. Those who for centuries have commanded love and imitation—Christ, Socrates, the martyrs; the tragic hero always; the warrior from Achilles to the Unknown Soldier—all are sacrificial victims, all resolve conflict by dying and through death ensure that the spirit they spoke or fought for shall not perish. The pattern is so honored and familiar that a connection between heroism and death seems natural.

The struggle to survive, on the other hand, is felt to be suspect. We speak of "merely" surviving, as if in itself life were not worth much; as if we felt that life is justified only by things which negate it. The contradic-

3

tion is real; it goes to the root of how we envision death in relation to life, and I shall try to account for it. We may find, in the end, that the hero's death is appointed —that one of the functions of culture is to provide symbolic systems which displace awareness of what is terrible, and that through death the hero takes upon himself the condition of victimhood and thereby grants the rest of us an illusion of grace. Dying gods and sacrificial victims have regularly attended the rise of civilizations; and often, as in the case of Greek tragedy, societal well-being and ritual death seem inseparable. The problem now is that symbolic manipulations of consciousness no longer work. Death and terror are too much with us.

Men have always been ready to die for beliefs, sacrificing life for higher goals. That made sense once, perhaps; but no cause moves without live men to move it, and our predicament today—as governments know—is that ideas and ideologies are stopped by killing those who hold them. The "final solution" has become a usual solution, and the world is not what it was. Within a landscape of disaster, places like Auschwitz, Hiroshima or the obliterated earth of Indochina, where people die in thousands, where machines reduce courage to stupidity and dying to complicity with aggression, it makes no sense to speak of death's dignity or of its communal blessing. We require a heroism commensurate with the sweep of ruin in our time: action equal to situations in which it becomes less self-indulgent and more useful to live, to be there. History moves, times change, men find themselves caught up in unexpected circumstance. The grandeur of death is lost in a world of mass murder, and except for special cases the martyr and his tragic counterpart are types of the hero unfit for the darkness ahead. When men and women must live against terrible odds, when mere existence becomes miraculous, to die is in no way a triumph.

If by heroism we mean the dramatic defiance of superior individuals, then the age of heroes is gone. If we have in mind glory and grand gesture, the survivor is not a hero. He or she is anyone who manages to stay alive in body *and* in spirit, enduring dread and hopelessness without the loss of will to carry on in human ways. That is all. What this kind of struggle entails, and in what the survivor's "humanness" consists, are the joint themes of this book. They are also themes in important recent novels, and although in a strict sense I am concerned only with the experience of actual survivors, fiction serves here as it has always served: it provides images whose formal purity brings some part, at least, of the world's confusion to focus. Existence in extremity is not an easy subject. It is hard to approach and harder still to understand. Through fiction, however, some start can be made, some framework fixed which mediates the difference between that world and ours.

In novels by Camus and Malamud, accordingly, survival is represented as an action with a political outcome. Here the survivor is a protagonist in the classic sense, for by staying alive he becomes an effective agent in the fight against evil and injustice. The survivors in Solzhenitsyn's novels, on the other hand, change nothing. To keep life and decency intact is the limit of their achievement. But by choosing not only to live, but to live humanly, they take upon themselves the burden of an action requiring much will and courage, much clear-sightedness and faith in life.

One more distinction: because the traditional hero chooses to find consummation in death, he controls the condition for his fulfillment. The survivor's choice is not absolute in the same way. To stay alive is of course the whole point, but unlike those who die deliberately, the survivor can never be sure of success. Any day sickness or the whim of a vicious guard can cut short the struggle. That is one more circumstance the survivor must face. If he or she should die, it is the fight to live and not the manner of dying which matters. And finally there is this: in extremity, the bare possibility of survival is not enough. There must also be a move beyond despair and self-pity to that fierce determination which survivors call up in themselves. To come through; to keep a living soul in a living body.

The first condition of extremity is that there is no escape, no place to go except the grave. It is like a city under siege, Paris in 1870, Leningrad of the 900 days, or like the town of Oran in *The Plague:* "But once the town gates were shut, every one of us realized that all . . . were . . . in the same boat, and each would have to adapt himself to the new conditions of life" (61). So begins Camus' allegory of the extreme situation. New conditions become "normal conditions—in other words, the plague" (166); and this, in its immense power, is like "the slow, deliberate progress of some monstrous thing crushing out all upon its path" (163). The city becomes a "victim world," and the old order is transformed. Schools turn into hospitals, the stadium becomes a quarantine camp, streetcars are used as death wagons. This is a world in which living and dying are no longer held separate; in which the forms of life are determined by death.

The plague is ubiquitous and no place is safe. Death waits at home, in the street, on the stage; and slowly the condition of anti-life, because it cannot be veiled in myth or held in the balance of combat, becomes anti-human as well. Subject to this pressure and unable to draw inspiration from traditional forms of courage-in-adversity, the people of the town suffer general collapse. They despair, become selfish and mean; they will not face facts, and behave as if asleep. Confronted with a terror that has no foretellable end, they are reduced to helplessness. If they had been attacked by something on the human scale, an invasion of hostile neighbors for example, the citizens of Oran would have rallied to the cause and given their lives as the martyr and the patriot have always done. But the extreme situation is not an event, not a period of crisis with its proper beginning, middle and end. It is a state of existence which persists beyond the ability of men to alter or end it. And because there is no opportunity for one all-out effort, no single battle to be fought come what may, the honored forms of heroism fail as models for action and spiritual support. A sense of impotence prevails and dehumanization sets in. Against *this* enemy the people of the town see no way left to act.

Extremity requires an attitude which allows men and women to act, and thereby to keep faith in themselves as something more than victims. First of all, then, the survivor is not a victim merely. He refuses to see his victimization as total, fights it as best he can, and will not consent to death in any form. He will not, that is, accept the logic of the situation imposed upon him. So there are two kinds of people in *The Plague,* the "townspeople" and the "volunteers." Both react to the plague, the former on its terms, the latter on terms partially their own. The "townspeople" remain subject to necessity, at one with the situation destroying them. The "volunteers" respond to the same necessity, but by opposing it. They turn reaction into action self-directed, and in this way move far enough beyond death's rule to keep themselves intact as human beings. Rieux, Tarrou and their co-workers pit themselves against the plague, with no conviction of success, but only determined not to stand idle while others suffer. Together, therefore, they organize hygienic programs, they tend the stricken, they dispose of the dead. They work twenty hours a day amid the stench and agony of the dying, spending themselves in that endless, empty time of day upon day, without the encouragement of visible progress, without the hope of a positive end in sight, and always with the knowledge that death may win. They carry on all the same, because "they knew it was the only thing to do" (121).

It is plainly the human thing to do. In ordinary times, to protect the living, aid the sick and bury the dead are taken for granted as elementary forms of human activity. In extremity, however, simply continuing to do one's job as part of the human community becomes difficult to the point of heroism. Yet Camus insists that his protagonists are not heroic in a traditional sense. As Rieux puts it: "there's no question of heroism in all this. It's a matter of common decency. . . . Heroism and sanctity don't really appeal to me. . . . What interests me is being a man" (150, 231). Rieux's characteristic understatement serves to point up the humility, the hardminded realism and rejection of drama which are essential to the survivor's outlook. His is a matter-of-factness rooted in the knowledge that survival *depends* on staying human. That, in fact, is the great theme of *The Plague,* and although to be human under pressure takes extraordinary effort, there is really no alternative: "The only means of fighting a plague is—common decency" (150). Hard as it is, therefore, the survivor's struggle is without glamor or special destiny. Camus' "volunteers" are doing what anyone should do, and doing it simply to live. As Rieux concludes: "there was nothing admirable about this attitude; it was merely logical" (122).

The tragic hero finds in death a victory. Thereby he places himself beyond compromise, beyond the erosion of time, and the truth for which he stood is solemnized, pressed deep in the hearts of his audience through the drama of his sacrifice. He is proof of spirit's contempt for the flesh, and death itself becomes the confirmation of greatness. There is much to be admired in such a stance, but not in time of plague. For the survivor all things—himself, his works, the race of man—are painfully mortal, and when all are endangered there may be no audience to count on. Hemingway has said of the tragic hero that he is "destroyed but not defeated," implying a capacity to stand firm to the end. The survivor too stands firm; but for those who choose life, to die is to lose.

The Plague can be read as an account of France under Nazi occupation, and *The Fixer,* to which I now turn, is based on a notorious case of anti-Semitism (the Beiliss trial in Kiev in 1913). Camus and Malamud, each in a way peculiar to his art and personal experience, are responding directly to the climate of atrocity which like a leveling wind has touched and unsettled every aspect of existence in our century. Their vision is informed by genocide and the concentration camps, and it becomes particular through individuals caught up in events which threaten to destroy not only populations but the human spirit itself. "We're dealing nowadays," says Malamud's small hero, "with the slaughter of large numbers and it's getting worse" (258). Against an evil so vast, individual actions seem slight indeed, in no way victorious or spectacular, but not, for all that, without

intense significance. Individual men and women, either
alone or in concert with their fellows, must still be *there,*
in that place at that time, and by the fact of their existence be proof that no matter how bold and massive
the machinery of power becomes it does not prevail.

Yakov Bok leaves the pale, goes to Kiev, and finds
himself in the hands of his enemies, "unjustly accused,
helpless, unable to offer proof or be believed" (104).
His fate is like the larger fate of the Jews: "Overnight a
madman is born who thinks Jewish blood is water.
Overnight life becomes worthless. . . . So what can
Yakov Bok do about it?" (274). If he dies, nothing,
and that he will die is probable: "It was a natural thing
for prisoners to die in prison. They died like flies all over
Russia" (273). Accused of killing a Christian child, the
fixer is held for two years in prison where every pressure
against life and mind, short of outright murder, is in-
flicted upon him. With only a rabid anti-Semitism to
support its case, the government is afraid to bring him
to public trial. The alternative is to break his spirit and
obtain a confession, while at the same time arranging
conditions which will increase the probability of sickness and accident—in the hope that, once more, death
will resolve an otherwise unresolvable situation.

The fixer is held in isolation and has no sense of the
political situation, but he knows that if the government
should "prove" its case, the Black Hundreds will be
vindicated and pogroms will wring yet more blood from
his people. Against this possibility he will do what he
can. To die in prison would be to accept his role as
victim and confirm his appointed guilt. Therefore he
must stay alive, and by refusing to disappear in death,
force the government to bring him to trial. His mission,
he comes to see, is simply to survive: "Therefore he
must endure to the trial and let them confirm his inno-

cence by their lies. He has no future but to hold on, wait it out" (274).

To hold on and wait are imperatives which define the survivor's struggle, but against what? Against conditions opposed to life as we know it, conditions which civilization works to transcend and keep us, the lucky ones, from falling back into—random death and spiritual vacuum, physical anguish and empty time. The fixer lives in an unrelieved state of physical pain, enduring unmet needs for food, air, sanitation and light, as well as intenser moments of sickness and beating. His existence is a closed circuit of physical-spiritual erosion which the tragic hero, his moment of agony surpassed in the glory of death, knows little of. This is the undramatic, unglorified sorrow of the body, a permanent part of the human condition which most of us prefer to ignore in favor of "inner" suffering—as if mind and body were separate worlds. But pain which goes on and on seeps through body *and* mind, and in this as in other respects, survival inverts the values of civilization. Physical existence can no longer be dismissed as unworthy of concern. The body's will and the will of the spirit must join in common cause.

The survivor must personally oppose conditions which the edifice of civilization was built to transcend. Structured time, the blessing of a foundation for measure and purposive action, is one of civilization's great gifts. But in extremity the forms of time dissolve, the rhythms of change and motion are lost. Days pass, seasons, years pass and the fixer has no idea how long his ordeal will go on: "Time blew like a steppe wind into an empty future. There was no end, no event, indictment, trial" (238). His predicament is not a crisis, not a determinate span in a curve of significant time. It is an emptiness complete in itself, a suspension in the same-

ness of identical days which could last a year or a life-
time. Russian prisons have been notorious for lives spent
this way, and the fixer could remain in his cell, a young
man becoming an old man, without so much as a sentence to measure the waste of his life. The death of
time destroys the sense of growth and purpose, and
thereby undermines faith in the possibility that any good
can come from merely staying alive. This too the survivor must face and withstand.

Holding on, the fixer is repeatedly forced to recognize
that "whenever he had been through the worst, there was
always worse" (295). The spirit's element is space, and
among other things civilization is the creation of a
steady space in which our humanity can freely hatch and
thrive. It is a space of sustaining plenitude, a network
of meaning and interchange, the matrix of human communion. Certainly it is not an empty space, for nothing,
we are sure, can live in a vacuum. But for the fixer, the
emptiness of time is compounded by the emptiness of
total isolation. The one man with whom he communi-
cates is murdered, the only other men he sees are his
jailors. He has no contact with the world outside, no
sense of his plight as part of a larger whole. His life, his
suffering, seem severed from human community, and he
is forced to endure with the thought that "he suffers for
no one except himself" (240).

But as a man unjustly condemned, he *is* connected to
others, to the Jews first of all and then to men and wom-
en everywhere who like himself are the victims and
scapegoats of power. At first he insists that he is not a
"political person." But gradually his suffering brings
home to him the pain of all men in extremity, and he
comes finally to realize that when the exercise of power
includes the death of innocent people, "there's no such
things as an unpolitical man" (335). The "political

person," in the pure sense Malamud intends, is the man or woman conscious of the individual's implicit relation to the community of others, and therefore the person who takes intelligent action to make explicit and effective this vital connection of one to all. For the fixer, intelligent action means to survive and by his irreducible presence, by refusing to go away or be simply a victim, to force the government to expose itself by bringing him to trial.

Survivors do not choose their fate and would escape it if they could. They are trapped in a world of total domination, a world hostile to life and any sign of dignity or resistance—a world, finally, in which an anti-human order is maintained by the bureaucratic application of death. Here, to remain alive and human demands not only a certain kind of action, as we have seen, but also a radical shift in the sense of selfhood. Survivors are uncommonly conscious of limits and foundations, of the strength to be found in innocence, and especially of the sustaining power which life itself provides when all else has been stripped away. Precisely because it does not die or give up, the self comes upon itself and the ground of itself as it could never do while enjoying the delicate, efflorescing extensions of selfhood which civilization creates and fosters. From this experience comes a special integrity, a clearness of vision indispensable to those for whom, outwardly, helplessness and victimization are major facts of existence.

No novelist has described this kind of consciousness better than Solzhenitsyn. His survivor is the man in love with his people and their cause, the man who stood against the Nazi onslaught only to find himself thrown into a slave camp; this same man, helpless but unreconciled to his fate, determined to remain innocent and unbroken under conditions specifically devised to crush out life and spirit. His energies burn with the pointed fury of an extreme tension between the will to live and the will to remain pure—between an almost mystical thirst for life and an unwavering refusal to capitulate, sell out, or in any way become accessory to a system which reduces men to puppets and meat. He rejects the benefits of abdication and, powerless, chooses not to compromise. Thereby he becomes a sliver in the throat of power, and is proof, to himself and others who would join him, that men and women can sustain enormous damage and still go on as human beings.

Shukhov, the hero of *One Day in the Life of Ivan Denisovich,* is this kind of man. He has been unjustly imprisoned, and has lived through years of sub-zero weather without decent clothing or a warm place to sleep, rising each day before the sun to twelve hours of heavy labor on a starvation diet. He steers his life through sickness and exhaustion, through the random cruelty of camp procedure and the betrayal of fellow prisoners, and yet he is not broken: "even eight years as a convict hadn't turned him into a jackal—and the longer he spent at the camp the stronger he made himself" (142). Shukhov is willing to give way to other prisoners, to perform services for men he respects, but he will not make a deal with those in power, never inform, never do a favor for the cooks or ask one of them. He has developed the *zek*'s special ability to cheat the officials and camp regulations, by which he saves his strength and now and then gets an extra bowl of soup (these are major victories), but he will not cheat others in the same situation as himself. And through it all he maintains an elementary sense of self-respect: "Every nerve in his body was taut, all his longing was concentrated in that cigarette butt—which meant more to him now, it seemed, than freedom itself—but he would never lower himself . . . he would never look at a man's mouth" (40).

Due to his situation as much as to his character, Shukhov has come a long way in the wisdom of simplicity. He has learned to extract sharp satisfaction—a sense of animal well-being which saves him from self-pity and despair—from slight and infrequent moments of pleasure. Working with his squad to build a wall (the temperature is −17°), Shukhov is inspired to delight by the rhythm of the work and the interplay of skills. He enjoys the warmth which spreads through his body, and later, the firmer joy of a job well done. He has come to appreciate, deeply and to the full, every inch of life that transcends pain and hopelessness. By far the most important event in his life is food, and like all of Solzhenitsyn's characters, Shukhov has developed an extraordinary attitude toward the watered soup and black bread which sustain him. Eating becomes a small ritual, an experience which provides a physical ground for faith in the value of life. Soup-time is for Shukhov a "sacred moment," a revelation deep in the body's pleasure that, at bottom and in spite of everything, life is strong and worth its pain:

> Shukhov took off his hat and laid it on his knees. He tasted one bowl, he tasted the other. Not bad —there was some fish in it. . . .
> He dug in. First he only drank the broth, drank and drank. As it went down, filling his whole body with warmth, all his guts begun to flutter inside him at their meeting with that stew. Goo-ood! . . .
> And now Shukhov complained about nothing: neither about the length of his stretch, nor about

the length of the day, nor about their swiping another Sunday. This was all he thought about now:
we'll survive. We'll stick it out, God willing, till
it's over (136).

He eats his soup and bliss wells up like a benediction,
like an extravagant blessing, as though this second bowl,
tricked from the cooks, were life's finest gift. Shukhov
attains that rarest of moments, when a person is simply,
and against all evidence, happy to be alive. The importance of food to people starving is perhaps not easy
for us to imagine. It is even more difficult for us to
understand that this man's affirmation is made in the
middle of a concentration camp.

But the whole point of *One Day* is that such a man
exists in such a place. Surrounded by the inhumanity of
man and nature, Shukhov has made a life for himself,
with its gross imbalance of pain and pleasure, privation
and fulfillment. And to a slight but crucial degree it is
his life, affirmed anew in each violation of camp regulations, in each moment of pleasure. He knows, of
course, that *this* day was uncommon for luck, and that
pain is the substantial element in which he must live.
But he has come to terms with it, transcended his victimization by refusing self-pity or the temptation to hope
for anything but life itself, and then gone on to find what
goodness he can in the life he has. Like all survivors,
he has squarely faced the basic problems of existence in
extremity. The first is how not to despair. The second,
how to keep moral sense and dignity intact.

Like thousands of actual P.O.W.'s, Shukhov was sent to
the camps because during the war he had been captured
by the Germans. According to his interrogator, "he'd

surrendered to the Germans with the intention of betraying his country" (71). Millions of men and women under Soviet rule were imprisoned for similar—and similarly insane—reasons. In *The First Circle,* Gerasimovich becomes a *zek* for "intent to commit treason," Kagan for "failure to inform." These strictly imaginary crimes were defined and made real by *Article 58* of the penal code. Anyone who stood out, either by accident or decision, sooner or later could expect to be arrested —anyone incompatible with the system in which he or she was trapped. The Soviet camps were full of people arrested *because* they were innocent, because they would not cooperate with evil, because they possessed the integrity to think and judge for themselves. In *Cancer Ward* Kostoglotov and his fellow students get seven years plus exile: "We used to come together, court the girls, dance; but the boys also talked about politics. And about HIM. . . . In May, just before the examinations, we were all arrested, the girls too" (193).

When a government rules by force and falsehood, when people are murdered in great numbers and the prisons are jammed with men and women who even the interrogators know are innocent, then to escape involvement becomes impossible. Some work with the system, become murderers. Others—millions—become victims. Still others watch and pretend they do not see. Many men and women were swept into the Soviet camps by pure accident. They happened to be in the wrong place at the right time, they became part of a quota. But there was always an outside chance that if one stayed far enough in the background and was very quiet, one might be overlooked. In a totalitarian state which uses the threat of imprisonment to maintain its power, an element of choice thus arises. In *Cancer Ward* Shulubin, bitter because he saw and remained silent, quotes Push-kin:

> In this our age of infamy
> Man's choice is but to be
> A tyrant, traitor, prisoner;
> No other choice has he.

People still free must decide how much their "free-dom" is worth: how many lies they will live by, how far they will acquiesce while their neighbors are destroyed. The choice is always there. Those arrested for "failure to inform" might have decided to go along with the police that far at least. Kostoglotov and his friends did not have to discuss politics, did not have to criticize HIM. "If one is forever cautious, can one remain a hu-man being?" (3). So thinks Innokenty Volodin, the young diplomat in *The First Circle* whose simple act of humanity will send him into the camps. In extremity that question is everyman's. Each must decide how he or she will reconcile the desire for life and comfort with the desire for purity and self-respect. In relation to this choice, each character in Solzhenitsyn's world takes his or her position on a scale of moral being which reaches from monstrosity to sainthood.

The low end is occupied by men in positions of authority: petty bureaucrats, state officials, Stalin first of all. Minister of State Security Abakumov, for example, is the model of official success: "it turned out that Ab-akumov conducted interrogations effectively; his long arms were an asset when it came to smashing people in the face" (72). His talent has brought him close to Stalin, increasing the chance of a bullet in the neck, and his dread filters down through the hierarchy, each man beneath the heel of the man above him. All the ministers, bureaucrats, jailors, etc. who serve the system comprise the "they" to which the *zeks* refer, men without character or depth, the product of the machine they service. And although their safety is never assured, they are one kind of survivor, a kind to be found in the camps as well. Siromankha, king of the camp informers in *The First Circle,* is a kind of survivor whose behavior is legendary. He is one of "those who, as camp guards, could club their countrymen in the face; those who, as bread cutters and cooks, could eat the bread of others who were starving" (466). Plainly, there is more than one way to survive, and a point after which the heroism of survival turns into its opposite. The distinction is between those who live at any price, and those who suffer whatever they must in order to live humanly. As Solzhenitsyn sums it up, "The wolfhound is right and the cannibal is wrong" (401).

There are, then, prisoners who have come into the camps not because they gave up, but because they refused to give up. They are there because they persist in the desire to preserve their innocence and to keep themselves intact as human beings. This desire, and the possibility of this choice, is the axis of concern in *The First Circle.* Foremost among Solzhenitsyn's band of survivors, and the center of moral intelligence in the novel, is Gleb Nerzhin, "a prisoner in his fifth year in harness who never hurries because he expects only worse from what lies ahead" (37). Like Solzhenitsyn himself, Nerzhin was arrested at the front for private criticism of Stalin, and given a ten-year term. He is a mathematician, brought to the special prison at Mavrino after four years of labor in the northernmost camps. Mavrino, by comparison, is a godsend: "Hands not flayed with work. Fingers not frozen" (42). Here the *zeks* are scientists and technicians, but they are forced to work on the re-

finement of a special technology—devices which will
serve the growth of totalitarian control. Most of them
only pretend to work, but anyone who directly refuses
to cooperate is certain to be in the next transport back
to the camps, which means—

> Perhaps he will not arrive at his destination. In a
> cattle car he may die either of dysentery or of hun-
> ger, because the zeks will be hauled along for six
> days without bread. Or the guard may beat him
> with a hammer because someone has tried to es-
> cape. Or, at the end of the journey in an unheated
> car, they may toss out the frozen corpses of the
> zeks like logs (558).

At Mavrino Nerzhin is forced to work, but he does not
give himself to the purpose imposed upon him. His desk
is piled with books and folders, but "in fact, it was all
a false front" (19). His real work is a collection of
notes in which he analyzes the failure of the Revolu-
tion—how, that is, history purifying itself came to result
in concentration camps. But then he is called before the
officials and asked to volunteer for a special project, and
this he will not do. If he were to agree, he might earn
his release. His refusal, on the other hand, "was certain
to result, perhaps very soon, in a long and arduous
journey to Siberia or the Arctic, to death or to a hard
victory over death" (65). Other prisoners, like Rubin
and Sologdin, decide to work for their freedom (and
Solzhenitsyn allows them a sympathetic understanding).
But Nerzhin is uncompromising; he will keep himself
pure and take his chances. As soon as the decision is
made his spirit begins to shore its strength, drawing on
the survivor's special wisdom:

Nerzhin . . . was now thinking that only the first year of camp could finish him, that he had achieved a completely different tempo, that he would not try to scramble into the ranks of the goldbrickers, that he would not be afraid of camp labor, but would slowly, with an understanding of life's depths, go out for morning line-up in his padded jacket smeared with plaster or fuel oil and tenaciously drag through the twelve-hour day——and so on, for the whole five years remaining until the end of his term. Five years is not ten. One can last five (136).

That is the survivor's predicament: like the "volunteers" in *The Plague*, he must be prepared to run risks which keep him alive by bringing him closer to death. The odd thing is that Nerzhin expects to gain in strength and in knowledge by an existence so radically pared down——as if *there*, at the absolute limit of body and soul, truths might be found on which a human being may firmly build. "Camp life," Solzhenitsyn tells us, "exceeds in its ruthlessness anything known of the lives of cannibals and rats" (208). But at the same time he speaks of "the harsh apprenticeship of camp" (388). To what can that refer, if not to the apprenticeship of one's own soul, to the crystallization of that essence all men and women share but seldom realize or even acknowledge? As Nerzhin puts it, "one must try to temper, to cut, to polish one's soul so as to become *a human being*" (389). That recalls Shukhov: "the longer he spent at the camp the stronger he made himself." It seems clear that the ordeal of survival becomes, at least for some, an experience of growth and purification.

By virtue of the extraordinary demands made upon men and women in extremity, their struggle to live humanly involves a process of becoming more——essentially, firmly—human. Not the humanness of refinement and proliferation, of course, but of the fundamental knowledge of good and evil, and of the will to stand by this knowledge, on which all else depends. Nerzhin says: "I had no idea what good and evil were, and whatever was allowed seemed fine to me. But the lower I sink into this inhumanly cruel world, the more I respond to those who, even in such a world, speak to my conscience" (515). For this kind of survivor, the way down is the way up.

Like other types of the hero, survivors take their stand directly on the line, but they are unique in that they *stay* there. And it is there, in the balance of being and non-being, that their peculiar freedom becomes real and effective. Their vision is not clouded by sheltering illusions; they do not suddenly, in the ambush of crisis, discover their mortality, for in order to remain alive they must at every moment acknowledge the centrality of death. This familiarity has not failed to breed a proper contempt: survivors may be killed, but as long as they live they will not be afraid. And closer to death, survivors are rooted more urgently in life than most of us. Their will to survive is one with the thrust of life itself, a strength beyond hope, as stubborn as the up-surge of spring. In this state a strange exultation fills the soul, a sense of being equal to the worst. And as long as they live, survivors *are* equal to the worst. This, final-ly, is the attitude of those *zeks*—Nerzhin, Gerasimovich and their friends—who at the end of *The First Circle* are shoved into a meat truck and shipped off to the camps:

Concentrating on the turns the van was making, the zeks fell silent.

Yes, the taiga and the tundra awaited them, the

record cold of Oymyakon and the copper excavations of Dzhezkazgan; pick and barrow; starvation rations of soggy bread; the hospital; death. The very worst.

But there was peace in their hearts.

They were filled with the fearlessness of those who have lost *everything,* the fearlessness which is not easy to come by but which endures (579).

Having fought against the Nazi invasion, Solzhenitsyn's survivors are also soldiers, and that is how they think of themselves as day by day they withstand extremity with the modest tactics which keep them alive. "A soldier gets along best on the defensive" (89), says Kostoglotov in *The Cancer Ward;* and in fact the survivor's struggle is very much like guerrilla warfare—"tactical offensives within the strategic defense," as Mao Tse-tung defined it (157). But the survivor's enemy is death, and in the end he is a soldier who can never hope for more than small and temporary victories. The cancer ward is death's home field, and those who find themselves there have no thought but to survive, to employ any medical tactic which may strengthen their defense. They fight as best they can, but since death will not retreat, they must come to terms with their situation so as to live beyond fear and despair: "In the face of death, in the face of the striped panther of death who had already lain down beside him, in the same bed, Vadim, as a man of intellect, had to find a formula for living" (293). Kostoglotov's answer is to live as the soldier lives: aware of danger and ready to die, yet putting up the longest fight possible, and regarding all men kindly but without pity as brothers in a losing war.

This hardness of the living heart is something a man

like Kostoglotov cannot do without. After the war he
entered the university, but before his life could begin to
take shape he was arrested and sent to the camps. After
that came exile, and then cancer, so we cannot avoid
the impression that Kostoglotov, still in his thirties, is
an old man. The pathos of his situation is that, on the
verge of death, he is a man who never had a life—"A
river that doesn't go anywhere, that haphazardly gives
away all its best water and power along the way"
(345). He has survived years of incredible hardship,
missed death by a hair's breadth, only to find, not the
tree of life flaming with promise and budding fruits, but
an implacable cancer which will soon shut life from
him. Kostoglotov thirsts for fulfillment with a fierceness
equaled only by his despair of attaining it. And having
acquired in the camps "the ability to shake off all but
the main thing" (170), he comes at last to the humblest
kind of hope: "I want to live for a bit without guards
and without pain, and that's the limit of my dreams"
(345).

This is as much as he can hope for from treatment
in the cancer ward:

> . . . not for a complete new life, but for an extra
> portion, like the make-weight end of a loaf fast-
> ened onto the main part of the ration, a twig stuck
> through the two to hold them together—part of
> the same ration, but a separate piece (565).

The image here comes from the camp experience, and
what it tells us is that the survivor only lasts. He does
not reach victory or a new existence but only some
"small, additional, added-on life" (566). And even that
has its price, for in extremity every moment of life is
purchased at exorbitant cost, forcing the survivor re-

peatedly to consider the balance of values. As Kostoglotov says, "I have often wondered before, and now particularly I wonder: What, after all, is the highest price one should pay for life? How much should one pay, how much is too much?" (346). The question is always there, and each turn of events requires a new answer. So it is when Kostoglotov enters the cancer ward. His chance for a bit more life depends on a hormone treatment which will deprive him of his virility, and this is the decision he must face: "To become a walking husk of a man—isn't that an exorbitant price? It would be a mockery. Should I pay it?" (346). And if he pays, what then?

> Whom shall I seek, with whom share
> The heavy-hearted joy of my survival?

In this small verse the whole of his fate is expressed. We can suppose that this lusty man would once have led a simple fruitful life, shared with the woman he has come to love. But now he must continue to live against encroaching cancer with the knowledge that he has lost everything; that love and work, children, life ripening within, will not be his to try. But he does choose to live, once more giving up a part of himself in order to preserve what he calls "the main thing." He will not stop now, because after the camps he cannot, in this last extremity, negate the only meaning his life has had; and because to continue to live, even for a few months, is worth it absolutely.

Survivors *choose* life, and the basis of their choice is apparent in the happiness of Kostoglotov's final walk through the city—his rapport with the teeming life and motion around him, the intense relish with which he eats some roasted meat, the tender gratitude he feels

toward Vega for her love. It is a wonderful day, and
the wisdom of his deep delight is evident: "Even if next
spring never came, even if this was the last, it was one
extra spring! And thanks be for that!" (571). Like
Shukhov and like Nerzhin, he is able to respond to life's
least gift with a fullness of joy which is, finally, greater
and more powerful than hope. That is the survivor's
small but invaluable return. In this state of mind Kostoglotov leaves the cancer ward in search of a flowering
apricot tree. Not to possess it, but only for a moment's
time to behold it, and allow the beauty of its delicate
blossoming to confirm the enduring *Yes* he has so often
and at such cost said to life.

Then back into exile. He boards the train, finds a
place in the baggage rack, and settles for the journey
thinking: "Others had not survived. He had survived"
(615). That is all. Kostoglotov is a man without hope,
but even so, he has lived as long as he could, without
damage to his innocence, without harm to others. And
in this effort—to carry on when ordinary avenues of
life are closed and death lies visible ahead—the survivor reaches his limit. In the end he has nothing, nothing at all but this short reprieve, this extra life free and
his own. The loss of particular hope opens on the power
of life in itself, something unexpectedly uncovered
when the spirit is driven down to its roots and through
its pain is brought to a stillness and finality which—as
men once said—surpasses understanding. For survivors
that is enough.

THE WILL TO BEAR WITNESS

Rejected by mankind, the condemned do not go so far as to reject it in turn. Their faith in history remains unshaken, and one may well wonder why. They do not despair. The proof: they persist in surviving—not only to survive, but to testify.

The victims elect to become witnesses.

ELIE WIESEL
One Generation After

During the terrible years of Yezhovshchina I spent seventeen months in the prison queues in Leningrad. One day someone recognized me. Then a woman with lips blue with cold who was standing behind me, and of course had never heard of my name, came out of the numbness which affected us all and whispered in my ear—(we all spoke in whispers there):

"Can you describe this?"

I said, "I can!"

Then something resembling a smile slipped over what had once been her face.

ANNA AKHMATOVA
Requiem

TO COME from fiction to documents is to move from an ideal lucidity to the dense anguish of men and women telling as straightforwardly as they know how the story of what they saw and endured in their passage through the concentration camps. Their testimony is given in memory, told in pain and often clumsily, with little thought for style or rhetorical device. The experience they describe, furthermore, resists the tendency to fictionalize which informs most remembering. We have accepted the idea that when the past is described the narrator selects and arranges, points up and slides over, maneuvering the facts to produce an acceptable image. And no doubt that is true for men and women in civilized circumstances, where there is always more than one level of meaning to choose from, more than one way to view the facts. But the world survivors speak of has been so rigidly shaped by necessity, and so completely shared—almost all survivors say "we" rather than "I"—that from one report to the next the degree of consistency is unusually high. The facts lie embedded in a fixed configuration; fixed, we may come to believe, by the nature of existence when life is circumscribed by death.

Men and women are happy in a multitude of ways, but in sorrow's deepest moments all are one. The experience of extremity issues always in the same need and pain, always in what Barrington Moore, Jr., has called "the unity of misery" (11). We may prefer to ignore the world's anguish, and those who must bear it have seldom been articulate. But radical suffering, as Moore observes, "has been the lot of a very large portion of humanity for nearly all of recorded history. The inarticulateness of the victims, very few of whom have left any records, has to a great extent masked its extent" (11-12). By "suffering" he does not mean embattled love or yearning for God, but the gross pain of flesh and of physically uprooted lives. The First World War was the first mass disaster experienced by large numbers of people who were literate and therefore able to leave records. And what they reveal of human struggle is not high cause and glorious downfall, but defilement and dazing fear, dumb hurt and bodies rotting in mud.

In the concentration camps there was an even wider margin of literacy, and many men and women returned who if not sophisticated were certainly articulate enough to give clear accounts. Through survivors a vast body of literature has thus come into being—diaries, novels, documentary reports, simple lists and fragments, books in many languages, which all tell one story. This kind of writing is unusual for the experience it describes, but also for the desire it reveals to remember and record. The testimony of survivors is rooted in a strong need to make the truth known, and the fact that this literature exists, that survivors produced these documents—there are many thousands of them—is evidence of a profoundly human process. Survival is a specific kind of experience, and "to survive as a witness" is one of its forms.

What happened in the Warsaw Ghetto is known in detail because many people made it their job to write down what they saw and experienced. The *Warsaw Diary* of Chaim A. Kaplan is one example. From September 1, 1939, when Hitler invaded Poland, until the afternoon of August 4, 1942, when Kaplan was sent to the extermination camp at Treblinka, he set down each day's disasters in a child's copybooks. At different moments he refers to his job as a "duty," as a "mission," and as a "sacred task." "My utmost concern," he tells us, "is for hiding my diary so that it will be preserved for future generations" (395). This thrust of urgent purpose never left him. He describes it, at one point, as "a flame imprisoned in my bones, burning within me, screaming: Record!" (144). Kaplan's sense of this command was absolute, and neither periods of desperation nor the coming of death could weaken the almost mystical compulsion which governs his work: "But this despair does not last forever. The spirit of dedication which had left me in my moments of spiritual agony returns, as though some hidden force were ordering me: Record!" (233).

Why this feeling was so strong, or what he expected to achieve, are issues Kaplan does not discuss. What is clear, however, is his passionate will to preserve the memory of the horror he has witnessed. And this desire was not his alone. When men and women are forced to endure terrible things at the hands of others—whenever, that is, extremity involves moral issues—the need to remember becomes a general response. Spontaneously they make it their business to record the evil forced upon them. "The drive to write down one's memoirs is powerful," observes Emmanuel Ringelblum in his *Notes from the Warsaw Ghetto;* "even young people in labour camps do it" (133). "In spite of hunger, illness and privation, there was a compulsion to record this period in all its details" (83), says David Wdowinski in *And We Are Not Saved.* Those caught were shot, but that did not keep Ringelblum and his friends from organizing a clandestine group whose job was to gather information for deposit in a secret archive (much of which survived). Here, and in similar situations, survival and bearing witness become reciprocal acts.

For most survivors the chance to speak comes later. To bear witness is the goal of their struggle. This was true, certainly, for many in the concentration camps—as Alexander Donat, for example, makes clear in *The Holocaust Kingdom*. Donat fought in the Warsaw Ghetto uprising, then went through Maidanek, Auschwitz and Dachau. From the start he had one intention: "I felt I was a witness to disaster and charged with the sacred mission of carrying the Ghetto's history through the flames and barbed wire until such time as I could hurl it into the face of the world. It seemed to me that this sense of mission would give me the strength to endure everything" (183). Donat's desire to be a witness was so strong that this task became, finally, the essence of his identity as a survivor:

> I was now an old-timer, resistant to pain and cold; inured to beating, opprobrium and heavy labor; insensitive to pain and unhappiness. All I retained was the newspaperman's greedy curiosity, the desire to see and find out everything, to engrave in my memory this Dantesque world (253).

Donat had been a journalist before the war, but the impulse he describes is not limited to men and women of that profession. "While still in the camp," says Halina Birenbaum in *Hope Is the Last To Die*, "I decided that if I lived to see liberation, I would write down everything I saw, heard and experienced" (244). In *Survival in Auschwitz* Primo Levi recalls his drift toward fatal indifference, and the moment when a simple expression of care pulled him back together: "Stein-lauf, a man of good will, told me . . . that even in this place one can survive, and therefore one must want to survive, to tell the story, to bear witness" (36).

The survivor's aim, as Margarete Buber says in *Under Two Dictators,* is "to let the world know" (xii). Each piece of testimony by a survivor answers this need. Behind the individual witness, futhermore, lies the collective effort of many others. Here, too, there is plenty of evidence. Most dramatic, perhaps, is what happened at Treblinka. At the peak of operations, 15,000 men, women and children died there each day. Death on that scale took enormous labor, and toward the end, when the SS began to fear discovery, the mass graves were opened and the rotting bodies burned. All the actual work was done by several hundred prisoners called the *Sonderkommando.* Forced to wade through corpses, with SS bullets thinning their ranks, the work squads at Treblinka contained a core of men who managed to survive. And not just to save their skins. Against impossible odds they organized a resistance, they revolted, and on August 2, 1943, they burned down the camp.

It took months and months of preparation, cutting down the suicides, insisting that survival even in such a place is not without value. Their purpose—strong enough to lift the spirit from truly inhuman depths—was to destroy the camp and allow at least one man or woman to escape and bear the tale. "I found it most difficult to stay alive," says a survivor of Treblinka, "but I had to live, to give the world the story of this depravity, this bestial depravity" (Glatstein, 180). Meanwhile, the dead were being unearthed and burned, and soon the work squads too would go up in smoke. If that had come to pass, Treblinka would never have existed. The aim of the revolt was to ensure the memory of that place, and we know the story of Treblinka because forty survived.

In *Where Are My Brothers?* Sarah Berkowitz records a small incident: "One night a girl in our barrack started to scream terribly in her sleep. Within minutes all of us found ourselves screaming without knowing why" (82). Why? The place was Auschwitz; surely that was reason enough. The Holocaust produced an endless scream which, given time, has transmuted itself into the voice of many witnesses. This would seem, in fact, to be one of the primary aspects of the survival experience: the will to bear witness issues as a typical and in some sense necessary response to extremity. Confronting radical evil, men and women instinctively feel the desire to call, to warn, to communicate their shock. Terror dissolves the self into silence, but its aftermath, the spectacle of human mutilation, gives birth to a different reaction. Horror arises and in its presence men and women are seized by an involuntary outburst of feeling which is very much like a scream—sometimes, as we have seen, literally a scream. And in this crude cry the will to bear witness is born:

> This pitiful sound, which sometimes, goodness knows how, reaches into the remotest prison cell, is a concentrated expression of the last vestige of human dignity. It is a man's way of leaving a trace, of telling people how he lived and died. By his screams he asserts his right to live, sends a message to the outside world demanding help and calling for resistance. If nothing else is left, one must scream. Silence is the real crime against humanity (42-43).

These are the words of Nadezhda Mandelstam, whose *Hope Against Hope* stands second only to Solzhenitsyn's massive *GULAG* as an account of survival in Russia during the years of Stalin's terror. Her husband was Osip Mandelstam, one of Russia's finest poets. He made the mistake of writing a poem against Stalin, someone informed, and from then on their life was doomed and they knew it. After Mandelstam's disappearance into the camps, his wife lived on the move, leaving places sometimes hours before the police arrived to arrest her. She lied to get jobs, she lied to keep them. She watched those around her withdraw and grow silent, and she too said nothing. But all the time she was observing and remembering. And all the time the scream was growing. Nadezhda Mandelstam survived to testify, and in that purpose found strength to continue. The moral nature of this act, furthermore, shielded her from the debilitating fear which mere self-interest generates. To "survive as a witness," she came to believe, is *the* imperative of men in murderous times:

Most accounts of life in the camps appeared on first hearing to be a disconnected series of stories about the critical moments when the narrator nearly died but then miraculously managed to save himself. The whole of camp life was reduced to these highlights, which were intended to show that although it was almost impossible to survive, man's will to live was such that he came through nevertheless. Listening to these accounts, I was horrified at the thought that there might be nobody who could ever properly bear witness to the past. Whether inside or outside the camps, we had all lost our memories. But it later turned out that there were people who had made it their aim from the beginning not only to save themselves, but to survive as witnesses. These relentless keepers of the truth, merging with all the other prisoners, had bided their time—there were probably more such people in the camps than outside, where it was all too common to succumb to the temptation to make terms with reality and live out one's life in peace. Of course those witnesses who have kept a clear memory of the past are few in number, but their very survival is the best proof that good, not evil, will prevail in the end (379).

Death is compounded by oblivion, and the foundation of humanness—faith in human continuity—is endangered. The final horror is that no one will be left. A survivor of Dachau told me this:

The SS guards took pleasure in telling us that we had no chance of coming out alive, a point they emphasized with particular relish by insisting that after the war the rest of the world would not believe what happened; there would be rumors, speculations, but no clear evidence, and people would conclude that evil on such a scale was just not possible.

Without the past we have nothing to stand on, no context from which to organize the energies of moral vision. Against such possibilities survivors do what they can. Facing man-made horror, their need becomes strong to remember and record—to ensure, through their own survival or the survival of their word, that out

of horror's very midst (from where else can it come?)
the truth shall emerge.

"There was," says Elie Wiesel in *One Generation After,*
"a veritable passion to testify for the future, against
death and oblivion, a passion conveyed by every possible means of expression"; he goes on to cite "accounts
told with childlike artlessness" and "precisely kept
ledgers of horrors," all of which "waver between scream
and silent anger" (53). In *Night,* his first book, Wiesel
describes the agony of his boyhood in Auschwitz, and
it is that experience which becomes central to the
spiritual position of the protagonists in later books,
novels like *The Accident* and *The Gates of the Forest,*
in which Wiesel attempts to interpret, not the experience itself, but the survivor's relation to it in retrospect.
Before all else, Wiesel has been concerned with the
problems of the survivor *as a witness.* In *One Generation After* he says: "All questions pertaining to Auschwitz lead to anguish. Whether or not the death of one
million children has meaning, either way man is negated
and condemned" (56). But if faith in humanity is no
longer possible, what then is the point of bearing witness? "Was it not a mistake to testify, and by that very
act, affirm . . . faith in man and word?" (15).
   Silence is the only adequate response, but the pressure of the scream persists. This is the obsessive center
of Wiesel's writing: his protagonists desire a silence
they cannot keep. In *The Oath* the members of a Jewish
community, awaiting the pogrom that will destroy them,
make a solemn promise never to reveal their fate; but
the sole survivor finds that such a silence is more than
he can bear. In *Beggar in Jerusalem* the hero crawls
out of a mass grave and makes his way to Israel where,

as witness, he becomes the necessary connection between past and future. Through him the silence speaks and the new spirit of resistance stays loyal to the suffering which was its birth. The conflict between silence and the scream, so prominent in Wiesel's novels, is in fact a battle between death and life, between allegiance to the dead and care for the living, which rages in the survivor and resolves itself in the act of bearing witness.

Silence, in its primal aspect, is a consequence of terror, of a dissolution of self and world that, once known, can never be fully dispelled. But in retrospect it becomes something else. Silence constitutes the realm of the dead. It is the palpable substance of those millions murdered, the world no longer present, that intimate absence—of God, of man, of love—by which the survivor is haunted. In the survivor's voice the dead's own scream is active. A man named Alexander Donat accidentally took the place of a man named Michael Berg in a death brigade; and Berg, in his capacity as witness, writes *The Holocaust Kingdom* in Donat's name. This is a primary source of the will to bear witness: the survivor allows the dead their voice; he makes the silence heard.

There is evidence of this impulse in most books by survivors. In *Eleven Years in Soviet Prison Camps*, Elinor Lipper speaks of

> . . . the silence of the Siberian graveyards, the deathly silence of those who have frozen, starved, or been beaten to death. This book is an attempt to make that silence speak (viii).

To speak in memory of the dead becomes a kind of "mandate," as in Olga Lengyel's *Five Chimneys:*

In setting down this personal record I have tried to carry out the mandate given to me by the many fellow internees at Auschwitz who perished so horribly. This is my memorial to them (208).

Eugene Heimler wrote *Night of the Mist* to fulfill a similar need:

There were things I had to do, words I had to speak, moments which I had to dissect in order to show the world what I had seen and lived through, on behalf of the millions who had seen it also— but could no longer speak. Of their dead, burnt bodies I would be the voice (191).

Statements like these suggest many things. Most evident is the survivor's compassion, and after that, his loyalty. He survived, others did not, but all were there together. He knows he did not come through alone. Nobody survived without help. Life in the camps was savage, and yet there was *also* a web of mutual aid and encouragement, to which all books by survivors testify. As we shall see, some minimal fabric of care, some margin of giving and receiving, is essential to life in extremity. In a literal sense, therefore, the survivor owes his life to his comrades.

This debt to the dead, furthermore, is reinforced by the special kind of identity which survivors share. In the camps men and women were reduced to a single human mass. They all looked alike—the same filthy rags, shaved heads, stick-thin festering bodies—and the same hurt and need was each one's lot. Survivors are not individuals in the bourgeois sense. They are living remnants of the general struggle, and certainly they know it. Firsthand accounts of life in the concentration camps almost never focus on the trials of the writer apart from his or her comrades, apart from the thousands of identical others whose names were never known. Books by survivors are invariably group portraits, in which the writer's personal experience is representative and used to provide perspective on the common plight. Survival is a collective act, and so is bearing witness. Both are rooted in compassion and care, and both expose the illusion of separateness. It is not an exaggeration, nor merely a metaphor, to say that the survivor's identity includes the dead.

And there is also this: in extremity men and women make a special promise among themselves, always implicit and often openly declared. Scrawled on the latrine wall in a Soviet camp was this inscription: "May he be damned who, after regaining freedom, remains silent" (Ekart, 12). Whoever comes through will take with him the burden of speaking for the others. Someone will survive and death will not be absolute. This small pledge, this gigantic demand, is intensely important to people facing extinction. In the survivor's own case, furthermore, it becomes a way to transcend the helplessness which withers hope and self-respect in the presence of so much affliction. Surrounded by suffering he cannot comfort or prevent, this much at least he *can* do: the deaths, the sorrow, the infinite dragging pain shall not be lost completely. In this way the survivor's relation to the dead is compounded and made final:

His [fate] had fallen on the side of life, and yet he felt that he would henceforth carry with him the fate of all these thousands. No, he had not gone through it "like a stone." The blood of all these sufferers had fused with his and made it dark and heavy with all their pain. . . .

"Do not forget us!" was their silent cry.
"Think of us! Help us! Do not forget us!"
No, he would never forget them (Wiechert, 125, 129).

Nevertheless, this concern for the dead has been taken as evidence of something irrational and therefore suspect in the survivor's behavior. Observers call it "survival guilt," a term much used and almost wholly negative in emphasis. The concept of guilt, in this respect, is most clearly developed in the work of Robert Lifton. In *Death in Life: Survivors of Hiroshima,* Lifton argues that guilt is the key to the survivor's mentality. The survivor has a "need to justify his own survival in the face of others' deaths" (35). This need arises from a "process of identification which creates guilt over what one has done to, or not done for, the dying while oneself surviving" (496). Lifton reduces the problem to the "inseparability of death and guilt" (499), and as might be expected, he focuses on "the survivor's tendency to incorporate within himself an image of the dead, and then to think, feel and act as he imagines they did or would" (496). I have tried to suggest some of the ways in which this "tendency to incorporate" comes about. In Lifton's view, however, the fact that living men and women insist upon remembering the dead is clear proof of neurosis. The aim of psychiatric treatment is adjustment, acceptance, forgetting—goals which constitute a condition the survivor rejects. The urgency of his need to bear witness puts him in open conflict with the system being imposed to explain away his behavior, and such opposition, from the psychiatric point of view, is further evidence of neurotic reaction.

Lifton's good will is evident, but as a psychiatrist he

can only assume that behavior as intense and single-minded as the survivor's is abnormal. Lifton's original focus on atomic-bomb survivors, furthermore, obscures an essential aspect of bearing witness which becomes clear in instances of protracted crisis. The will to bear witness arises early, not after guilt has had time to accrue, but during the *initial* stage of adjustment to extremity. This is an important point, and it is confirmed repeatedly in the descriptions survivors give of their experience. The following passage is from a survivor's letter to me, and plainly, the idea of a "task" precedes any notion of guilt:

> I feel no guilt in being a survivor, but I feel that I have a task to fulfill. We may call it the survivor task, and it is part of my ego ideal, not of my superego. This task crowded into my thinking when I participated for the first time at the roll call of the captives in the concentration camp Buchenwald thirty-four years ago when I had no guarantee whatsoever that I would be a survivor.

Another survivor, Leon Thorne, began *Out of the Ashes* in hiding, before he was captured and sent to the camps: "I dare not hope that I shall live through this period, but I must work as though my words *will* come through. I shall act and write as though there were hope for me" (13).

The survivor's behavior looks different when seen in terms of a "task," and Lifton too has noticed this. In *History and Human Survival* he refers to "the survivor's intense concern with historical record" (197); and although the "sense of special mission characteristic of survivors" is still explained by "the need to render significant the deaths they have seen" (204), Lifton's em-

phasis is now on a positive outcome. He wishes to
retain the concept of guilt, but—as in the following
remarks from an article in *Partisan Review*—finally he
wants to suggest a new way of thinking about it: "although as a psychiatrist I was brought up to look upon
guilt as a profound problem within neurosis, as indeed
it can be, one comes in certain situations to value it as
a process" (518). This, in turn, leads to the formulation
of an "energizing or animating guilt" (517), and ulti-
mately to a redefinition of survival guilt as "the anxiety
of responsibility" (519). At which point—and this is the
conclusion I draw from Lifton's work—the idea of
guilt transcends itself. As the capacity for response to
deeds and events; as care for the future; as awareness
of the interdependency of human life, it becomes simply conscience.

Ernest A. Rappaport has reached a similar conclusion. Drawing on personal experience (he was in Buchenwald) and on years of psychiatric work with survivors
of the Nazi camps, Rappaport argues that their experience was so radically unique that the theory of neurosis
is inadequate to deal with it. Much of their psychological difficulty is an outcome of the social resistance they
encounter when they do not go along with "the preferred attitude of forgetting." Which is to say that apart
from the idea of survival guilt, there is still the problem
of its usage, of how we deploy it as a defense.

The "world" to which survivors speak is very much
a part of their condition as witnesses. They speak *for*
someone, but also *to* someone, and the response they
evoke is integral to the act they perform. And here an
unexpected ambiguity arises. As a witness the survivor
is both sought and shunned; the desire to hear his truth
is countered by the need to ignore him. Insofar as we
feel compelled to defend a comforting view of life, we

tend to deny the survivor's voice. We join in a "conspiracy of silence," and undermine the survivor's authority by pointing to his guilt. If he is guilty, then perhaps it is true that the victims of atrocity collaborate in their own destruction; in which case blame can be imputed to the victims themselves. And if he is guilty, then the survivor's suffering, all the sorrow he describes, is deserved; in which case a balance between *that* pain and our own is restored.

Strategies like these are commonly employed against survivors. Most simply, of course, the imputation of guilt is a transfer from spectator to victim. People living safe and at ease are understandably disturbed; they are not, as civilized beings, prepared for what the survivor has to say. But the operation of denial runs deeper. Refusal to acknowledge extremity is built into the structure of existence as we, the lucky ones, know it. More perhaps than we care to admit, spiritual well-being has depended on systems of mediation which transcend or otherwise deflect the sources of dread. In the beginning, Genesis tells us, the earth was "without form and void." Out of nothing the human world was made, out of nothingness and terror. Man's ascent to dominion depended on mechanisms which deny, symbolically if not in fact, those primal negations of human value which we would rather ignore. Too close a knowledge of vulnerability, of evil, of human insufficiency, is felt to be ruinous. And therefore we assert that death is *not* the end, the body is *not* the self. The world is *not* a film upon the void, and virtue is *not* without Godhead on its side. So too with the survivor. The ostracism of outsiders, of bearers of bad news, is a very old practice. In order to gain momentum the human enterprise bought time and assurance by taking refuge in myth, in numbers, in any makeshift strategy of distance or denial.

But what was wisdom once is not so now. The gates of pearl have turned to horn, and the appearance of the survivor suggests—indeed this is his message—that we embrace illusion at our peril.

The survivor is ignored for at least one other reason. Since the middle of the nineteenth century, suffering has come to be equated with moral stature, with spiritual depth, with refinement of perception and sensibility. I can only guess at the sources of this idea: the Christian belief in salvation through pain; Kierkegaard's emphasis on despair and Nietzsche's on the abyss; and not least, the Marxist celebration of the oppressed and down-trodden. The roots are manifold, but the net result is simple: the more poignant one's own suffering (or so the argument goes), the more one rises superior to others, the more authentic one becomes. Then too, if dross turns to gold, one's own private hurt is easier to bear. A prominent scholar (his speciality is Dickens) told me that the trouble with characters in Solzhenitsyn's novels is that they do not seem to suffer—as if open pain were possible in *their* shoes. Odd as this sounds, there is among us an envy of suffering. It increases with education, and it reveals the bitterness felt when history renders our own pain trivial. But of course, to put a value on suffering is something only the happy few can afford. One of the strongest themes in the literature of survival is that pain is senseless; that a suffering so vast is completely without value *as suffering*.

The survivor, then, is a disturber of the peace. He is a runner of the blockade men erect against knowledge of "unspeakable" things. About these he aims to speak, and in so doing he undermines, without intending to, the validity of existing norms. He is a genuine transgressor, and here he is made to feel real guilt. The world to which he appeals does not admit him, and since he has looked to this world as the source of moral order, he begins to doubt himself. And that is not the end, for now his guilt is doubled by betrayal—of himself, of his task, of his vow to the dead. The final guilt is not to bear witness. The survivor's worst torment is not to be able to speak.

Life lives upon life. That is a truth which civilized people may choose to ignore, but which the survivor must face at every turn. We live, all of us, in a realm of mutual sacrifice, and it seems possible that those of us in the civilized state—where victimization is selective— accrue greater guilt than men and women trapped in open horror, where life's cost is general and not borne by any one person or class apart from the rest. Here in particular the survivor's experience qualifies what is called "collective" or "metaphysical" guilt. In *The Question of German Guilt,* Karl Jaspers put it this way:

> Metaphysical guilt is the lack of absolute solidarity with the human being as such—an indelible claim beyond morally meaningful duty. This solidarity is violated by my presence at a wrong or a crime. It is not enough that I cautiously risk my life to prevent it; if it happens, and if I was there, and if I survive where the other is killed, I know from a voice within myself: I am guilty of being still alive (71).

In *The Reawakening,* Primo Levi refers to this same feeling as

> . . . the shame . . . the just man experiences at an-other man's crime; the feeling of guilt that such a crime should exist, that it should have been intro-duced irrevocably into the world of things that

were hungry and they tore at their skeletal bodies with the emaciated hands covered in pus and dirt. They were beyond help. The SS guards denied them the mercy of shooting them all at once. Only three or four were called out daily to be shot. . . .

For days I couldn't swallow even a crumb of bread. The horror I lived through watching this agony will remain with me to the end of my days. Later I saw thousands of my fellow prisoners die from rifle shots, but even that could not compare with the terrible and unspeakable ordeal of the Stuthofers (Weiss, 188-89).

We will not understand the survivor's behavior apart from its context. That is the context.

The survivor preserves his life, but also his humanness, against a situation in which, at every turn, decency seems stupid or impossible. He anchors himself in the moral purpose of bearing witness, and thereby he maintains, in himself and in the action he performs, an integrity which contradicts the savagery surrounding him. His task is like one of those small rocks to which vast sea-plants hold upon the ocean floor—a point of stability and rooted strength against the brunt of each day's peril. In the introduction to his book of camp sketches, Alfred Kantor remarks not only upon his "overwhelming desire to put down every detail," but also on the saving grace of an activity like this:

My commitment to drawing came out of a deep instinct of self-preservation and undoubtedly helped me to deny the unimaginable horrors of

life at that time. By taking on the role of an "observer" I could at least for a few moments detach
myself from what was going on in Auschwitz and
was therefore better able to hold together the
threads of sanity (unpaged).

A purpose of this kind, moreover, remains undimin-
ished through time—years in some cases—because it is
integral to the survivor's situation. Its source is in the
moral emotion which horror provokes, a response intensified rather than weakened by the accumulation of
detail.

Horror arises from the visible wreckage of moral and
physical being. We instinctively feel that a mangled
body reveals a mangled soul, and that is an accurate
perception when we are dealing, as now, with the spiritual consequences of torture and extermination. In the
presence of things which negate all claim to life and
value—the bomb-scapes, the death-stench, the ditches
of gunned-down children—mind and flesh recoil in a
single expression of shock. The whole body screams, and
this "last vestige of human dignity," as Nadezhda Mandelstam suggested, is life's own cry of dread and care, of
recognition and refusal and appeal to resistance. On the
surface men go numb, but deeper down the scream is
there, "like a flame imprisoned in my bones," as Chaim
Kaplan put it. We tend to forget, or perhaps never knew,
how vigorous and strongminded the reaction to horror
can be.

This response, this *response-ability,* is what I wish to
call "conscience"—conscience in its social form; not the
internalized voice of authority, not the introspective
self-loathing of the famed "Puritan" or "New England"
conscience. And not remorse. If bearing witness were
an isolated private act, a purely subjective event, then

perhaps the theory of guilt would serve. But as we have
seen, the survivor's behavior is typical, and more, it is
integral to conditions which reach beyond personal involvement. Horrible events take place, that is the (objective) beginning. The survivor feels compelled to bear
witness, that is the (subjective) middle. His testimony
enters public consciousness, thereby modifying the
moral order to which it appeals, and that is the (objective) end. Conscience, in other words, is a social
achievement. At least on its historical level, it is the
collective effort to come to terms with evil, to distill a
moral knowledge equal to the problems at hand. Only
after the ethical content of an experience has been made
available to all members of the community does conscience become the individual "voice" we usually take
it for.

And like any witness, the survivor gives testimony in
situations where moral judgment depends on knowledge of what took place. Through him the events in
question are verified and their reality made binding in
the eyes of others. The survivor-as-witness, therefore,
embodies a socio-historical process founded not upon
the desire for justice (what can justice mean when genocide is the issue?), but upon the involvement of all
human beings in common care for life and the future.
"I want the world to read and to resolve that this must
never, never be permitted to happen again"—so concludes one survivor of Auschwitz (Lengyel, 208). "I
believe it is my duty," says another, "to let the world
know on the basis of first-hand experience what can
happen, what does happen, what must happen when
human dignity is treated with cynical contempt" (Buber,
xii). This is an attitude expressed often indeed by survivors. The assumption is that good and evil are only
clear in retrospect; that moral vision depends on assim-

ilation of the past; that man as man cannot dispense with memory. Wisdom depends on knowledge and it comes at a terrible price. It comes from consciousness of, and then response to, the deeds and events through which men have already passed. Conscience, as Schopenhauer put it, is "man's knowledge concerning what he has done" (104).

By now it should be evident that survival is an act whose value extends beyond the individual who survives. One way to make this clear is formulated by Hannah Arendt in the last pages of *Eichmann in Jerusalem:*

> It is true that totalitarian domination tried to establish these holes of oblivion into which all deeds, good and evil, would disappear, but just as the Nazis' feverish attempts, from June, 1942, on, to erase all traces of the massacres—through cremation, through burning in open pits, through the use of explosives and flame-throwers and bone-crushing machinery—were doomed to failure, so all efforts to let their opponents "disappear in silent anonymity" were in vain. The holes of oblivion do not exist. Nothing human is that perfect, and there are simply too many people in the world to make oblivion possible. One man will always be left alive to tell the story (211-12).

That one man or woman is enormously important. In Turkey in 1915, for example, a million people were massacred as part of a deliberate policy to rid the country of its Armenian population. There were pogroms in the cities; villages were burned; men, women and children were driven into the desert to starve and be cut down. Against this event very few voices were raised, so few, in fact, that when Hitler proposed the idea of genocide to his General Staff, he could dismiss world conscience by saying: "Who, after all, speaks today of the annihilation of the Armenians?" (Housepian, 61). Those who possess enormous means of destruction actually believe—and this is the logic of power in our time—that death is stronger than life. They believe that over bone and flesh a withering silence *can* be imposed.

We live in an age of genocide, a time of willingness to remove humanity in chunks from the path of this or that policy. Hitler set out to eliminate, among others, the Jews, the Poles, the Communists. Stalin began by crushing the Old Bolsheviks, the intellectuals, the recalcitrant peasantry, and then went on to spread a web of random death through the very fabric of social interdependence. In Hiroshima it was the population at large, and in Indochina all life—plant, human, animal—in the countryside. Genocide is a "crime against humanity" because it negates human values as such. Its victims are the innocent occupants of a certain amount of human space which henceforth will be empty. Mass murder is nothing new, of course. Incredibly enough, that argument is still used to dampen response to present atrocities. But when the administration of death becomes a bureaucratic procedure, when killing is computerized and efficiency is the only value left, then clearly we behold something more than the age-old disregard for life. In our time the outcome of power is hostility to life itself.

Modern history has created the survivor as a moral type. His or her special task, moreover, has become indispensable. When terrorism and mass murder prevail, there will be no sources of concrete information unless men and women survive. Conscience is not awakened by hearsay or surmise. Care for life beyond ourselves is born of personal knowledge, of the compassion which comes from knowing the fate of actual lives. In an age of total propaganda, furthermore, there is no way past falsehood and confusion, save in the testimony of eye-witnesses. Distrust of official information has produced a paralyzing hesitation toward facts not verified in direct experience. The stories survivors tell are limited, of course, but they possess the kind of certainty, wholly human and involved, that moral resistance needs. And in these ways survivors do have influence. The Left gradually withdrew support from Stalinist politics in many countries, in part because of books like Alexander Weissberg's *The Accused;* and the beginning of a libertarian movement in Russia is directly related to the survival and outspokenness of Solzhenitsyn.

Survivors do not bear witness to guilt, neither theirs nor ours, but to objective conditions of evil. In the literature of survival we find an image of things so grim, so heartbreaking, so starkly unbearable, that inevitably the survivor's scream begins to be our own. When this happens the role of spectator is no longer enough. But the testimony of survivors is valuable for something else as well. By the very fact that they came to be written, these documents are evidence that the moral self can resurrect itself from the inhuman depths through which it must pass. These books are proof that human heroism is possible. At the end of *Journey Through Hell,* Reska Weiss says: "I rejoice that I am alive and can bear witness to the miracle of survival" (253). The miracle is that she can make such a statement. Ordinary people, in no way different from ourselves, go through infernal agony; they keep moral sense and memory intact; and afterwards, they take upon themselves the pain of living through it again, in order to fix its detail and make it known.

EXCREMENTAL ASSAULT

As the column returns from work after a whole day spent in the open, the stench of the camp is overwhelmingly offensive. Sometimes when you are still miles away the poisoned air blows over you.

SEWERYNA SZMAGLEWSKA
Smoke over Birkenau

He had stopped washing a long time before . . . and now the last remnants of his human dignity were burning out within him.

GUSTAV HERLING
A World Apart

IT BEGAN in the trains, in the locked boxcars—eighty to a hundred people per car—crossing Europe to the camps in Poland:

> The temperature started to rise, as the freight car was enclosed and body heat had no outlet. . . . The only place to urinate was through a slot in the skylight, though whoever tried this usually missed, spilling urine on the floor. . . . When dawn finally rose . . . we were all quite ill and shattered, crushed not only by the weight of fatigue but by the stifling, moist atmosphere and the foul odor of excrement. . . . There was no latrine, no provision. . . . On top of everything else, a lot of people had vomited on the floor. We were to live for days on end breathing these foul smells, and soon we lived in the foulness itself (Kessel, 50-51).

Transport by boat, in the case of many Soviet prisoners, was even worse: "most people were seasick and they just had to vomit on those down below. That was the only way to perform their natural functions too" (Knapp, 59). From the beginning, that is, subjection to filth was an aspect of the survivor's ordeal. In Nazi camps especially, dirt and excrement were permanent conditions of existence. In the barracks at night, for example, "buckets of excrement stood in a little passage by the exit. There were not enough. By dawn, the whole floor was awash with urine and feces. We carried the filth about the hut on our feet, the stench made people faint" (Birenbaum, 226). Sickness made things worse:

Everybody in the block had typhus . . . it came to Belsen Bergen in its most violent, most painful, deadliest form. The diarrhea caused by it became uncontrollable. It flooded the bottom of the cages, dripping through the cracks into the faces of the women lying in the cages below, and mixed with blood, pus and urine, formed a slimy, fetid mud on the floor of the barracks (Perl, 171).

The latrines were a spectacle unto themselves:

There was one latrine for thirty to thirty-two thousand women and we were permitted to use it only at certain hours of the day. We stood in line to get into this tiny building, knee-deep in human excrement. As we all suffered from dysentery, we could rarely wait until our turn came, and soiled our ragged clothes, which never came off our bodies, thus adding to the horror of our existence by the terrible smell which surrounded us like a cloud. The latrine consisted of a deep ditch with planks thrown across it at certain intervals. We squatted on these planks like birds perched on a telegraph wire, so close together that we could not help soiling one another (Perl, 33).

Prisoners lucky enough to work in one of the camp hospitals, and therefore able to enjoy some measure of privacy, were not thereby exempt from the latrine's special horror: "I had to step into human excreta, into urine soaked with blood, into stools of patients suffering from highly contagious diseases. Only then could one reach the hole, surrounded by the most inexpressible dirt" (Weiss, 69). The new prisoner's initiation into camp life was complete when he "realized that there was no toilet paper"—

. . . that there was no paper in the whole of Auschwitz, and that I would have to "find another way out." I tore off a piece of my scarf and washed it after use. I retained this little piece throughout my days in Auschwitz; others did likewise (Unsdorfer, 102).

Problems of this kind were intensified by the fact that, at one time or another, *everyone* suffered from diarrhea or dysentery. And for prisoners already starved and exhausted, it was fatal more often than not: "Those with dysentery melted down like candles, relieving themselves in their clothes, and swiftly turned into stinking repulsive skeletons who died in their own excrement" (Donat, 269). Sometimes whole camp populations sickened in this way, and then the horror was overwhelming. Men and women soiled themselves and each other. Those too weak to move relieved themselves where they lay. Those who did not recover were slowly enveloped in their own decomposition: "Some of the patients died before they ever reached the gas chambers. Many of them were covered all over with excrement, for there were no sanitary facilities, and they could not keep themselves clean" (Newman, 39).

Diarrhea was a deadly disease and a source of constant befoulment, but it was also dangerous for another reason—it forced prisoners to break rules:

> Many women with diarrhea relieved themselves in soup bowls or the pans for "coffee"; then they hid the utensils under the mattress to avoid the punishment threatening them for doing so: twenty-five strokes on the bare buttocks, or kneeling all night long on sharp gravel, holding up bricks. These punishments often ended in the death of the "guilty" (Birenbaum, 134).

In another case a group of men were locked day after day in a room without ventilation or toilet facilities of any kind. Next to a window by which guards passed they discovered a hole in the floor. But to use it a man had to risk his life, since those caught were beaten to death. "The spectacle of these unfortunates, shaking with fear as they crawled on hands and knees to the hole and relieved themselves lying down, is one of my most terrible memories of Sachsenhausen" (Szalet, 51).

The anguish of existence in the camps was thus intensified by the mineral movement of life itself. Death was planted in a need which could not, like other needs, be repressed or delayed or passively endured. The demands of the bowels are absolute, and under such circumstances men and women had to oppose, yet somehow accommodate, their own most intimate necessities:

> Imagine what it would be like to be forbidden to go to the toilet; imagine also that you were suffering from increasingly severe dysentery, caused and aggravated by a diet of cabbage soup as well as by the constant cold. Naturally, you would try to go anyway. Sometimes you might succeed. But your

absences would be noticed and you would be beaten, knocked down and trampled on. By now, you would know what the risks were, but urgency would oblige you to repeat the attempt, cost what it might. . . . I soon learned to deal with the dysentery by tying strings around the lower end of my drawers (Maurel, 38-39).

With only one exception, so far as I know, psychoanalytic studies of the camp experience maintain that it was characterized by regression to "childlike" or "infantile" levels of behavior. This conclusion is based primarily on the fact that men and women in the concentration camps were "abnormally" preoccupied with food and excretory functions. Infants show similar preoccupations, and the comparison suggests that men and women react to extremity by "regression to, and fixation on, pre-oedipal stages" (Hoppe, 77). Here, as in general from the psychoanalytic point of view, context is not considered. The fact that the survivor's situation was itself abnormal is simply ignored. That the preoccupation with food was caused by literal starvation does not count; and the fact that camp inmates were *forced* to live in filth is likewise overlooked.

The case for "infantilism" had been put most forcefully by Bruno Bettelheim. A major thesis of his book *The Informed Heart* is that in extreme situations men are reduced to children; and in a section entitled "Childlike Behavior" he simple equates the prisoners' objective predicament with behavior inherently regressive. Bettelheim observes, for example—and of course this was true—that camp regulations were designed to transform excretory functions into moments of crisis. Prisoners had to ask permission in order to relieve themselves, thereby becoming exposed to the murderous whim of the SS guard to whom they spoke. During the twelve-hour workday, furthermore, prisoners were often not allowed to answer natural needs, or they were forced to do so *while* they worked and on the actual spot *where* they worked. As one survivor says: "If anyone of us, tormented by her stomach, would try to go to a nearby ditch, the guards would release their dogs. Humiliated, goaded, the women did not leave their places —they waded in their own excrement" (Zywulska, 67). Worst of all were the days of the death marches, when prisoners who stopped for any reason were instantly shot. To live they simply had to keep going:

> Urine and excreta poured down the prisoners' legs, and by nightfall the excrement, which had frozen to our limbs, gave off its stench. We were really no longer human beings in the accepted sense. Not even animals, but putrefying corpses moving on two legs (Weiss, 211).

Under such conditions, excretion does indeed become, as Bettelheim says, "an important daily event"; but the conclusion does not follow, as he goes on to say, that prisoners were therefore reduced "to the level they were at before toilet training was achieved" (132). Outwardly, yes; men and women were very much concerned with excretory functions, just as infants are, and prisoners were "forced to wet and soil themselves" just as infants do—except that infants are not forced. Bettelheim concludes that for camp inmates the ordeal of excremental crisis "made it impossible to see themselves as fully adult persons any more" (134). He does not distinguish between behavior in extremity and civilized behavior; for of course, if in civilized circumstances an adult worries about the state of his bowels, or sees the trip to the toilet as some sort of ordeal, then neurosis is evident. But in the concentration camps behavior was governed by immediate death-threat; action was not the index of infantile wishes but of response to hideous necessity.

The fact is that prisoners were *systematically* subjected to filth. They were the deliberate target of excremental assault. Defilement was a constant threat, a condition of life from day to day, and at any moment it was liable to take abruptly vicious and sometimes fatal forms. The favorite pastime of one *Kapo* was to stop prisoners just before they reached the latrine. He would force an inmate to stand at attention for questioning; then make him "squat in deep knee-bends until the poor man could no longer control his sphincter and 'exploded' "; then beat him; and only then, "covered with his own excrement, the victim would be allowed to drag himself to the latrine" (Donat, 178). In another instance prisoners were forced to lie in rows on the ground, and each man, when he was finally allowed to get up, "had to urinate across the heads of the others"; and there was "one night when they refined their treatment by making each man urinate into another's mouth" (Wells, 91). In Birkenau, soup bowls were periodically taken from the prisoners and thrown into the latrine, from which they had to be retrieved: "When you put it to your lips for the first time, you smell nothing suspicious. Other pairs of hands trembling with impatience wait for it, they seize it the moment you have finished drinking. Only later, much later, does a repelling odor hit your nostrils" (Szmaglewska, 154). And as we have seen, prisoners with dysentery commonly got around camp rules and kept from befouling themselves by using their own eating utensils:

> The first days our stomachs rose up at the thought of using what were actually chamber pots at night. But hunger drives, and we were so starved that we were ready to eat any food. That it had to be handled in such bowls could not be helped. During the night, many of us availed ourselves of the bowls secretly. We were allowed to go to the latrines only twice each day. How could we help it? No matter how great our need, if we went out in the middle of the night we risked being caught by the S.S., who had orders to shoot first and ask questions later (Lengyel, 26).

There was no end to this kind of degradation. The stench of excrement mingled with the smoke of the crematoria and the rancid decay of flesh. Prisoners in the Nazi camps were virtually drowning in their own waste, and in fact death by excrement was common. In Buchenwald, for instance, latrines consisted of open pits twenty-five feet long, twelve feet deep and twelve feet wide. There were railings along the edge to squat on, and "one of the favorite games of the SS, engaged in for many years," was to catch men in the act of relieving themselves and throw them into the pit: "In Buchenwald ten prisoners suffocated in excrement in this fashion in October 1937 alone" (Kogon, 56). These same pits, which were always overflowing, were emptied at night by prisoners working with nothing but small pails:

> The location was slippery and unlighted. Of the thirty men on this assignment, an average of ten

fell into the pit in the course of each night's work. The others were not allowed to pull the victims out. When work was done and the pit empty, then and then only were they permitted to remove the corpses (Weinstock, 157-58).

Again, conditions like these were not accidental; they were determined by a deliberate policy which aimed at complete humiliation and debasement of prisoners. Why this was necessary is not at first apparent, since none of the goals of the camp system—to spread terror, to provide slaves, to exterminate populations—required the kind of thoroughness with which conditions of defilement were enforced. But here too, for all its madness, there was method and reason. This special kind of evil is a natural outcome of power when it becomes absolute, and in the totalitarian world of the camps it very nearly was. The SS could kill anyone they happened to run into. Criminal *Kapos* would walk about in groups of two and three, making bets among themselves on who could kill a prisoner with a single blow. The pathological rage of such men, their uncontrollable fury when rules were broken, is evidence of a boundless desire to annihilate, to destroy, to smash everything not mobilized within the movement of their own authority. And inevitably, the mere act of killing is not enough; for if a man dies without surrender, if something within him remains unbroken to the end, then the power which destroyed him has not, after all, crushed everything. Something has escaped its reach, and it is precisely this something—let us call it "dignity"—that must die if those in power are to reach the orgasmic peak of their potential domination.

As power grows, it grows more and more hostile to

everything outside itself. Its logic is inherently negative, which is why it ends by destroying itself (a consolation which no longer means much, since the perimeter of atomic destruction is infinite). The exercise of totalitarian power, in any case, does not stop with the demand for outward compliance. It seeks, further, to crush the spirit, to obliterate that active inward principle whose strength depends on its freedom from entire determination by external forces. And thus the compulsion, felt by men with great power, to seek out and destroy all resistance, all spiritual autonomy, all sign of dignity in those held captive. It was not enough just to shoot the Old Bolsheviks; Stalin had to have the show trials. He had to demonstrate publicly that these men of enormous energy and spirit were so utterly broken as to openly repudiate themselves and all they had fought for. And so it was in the camps. Spiritual destruction became an end in itself, quite apart from the requirements of mass murder. The death of the soul was aimed at. It was to be accomplished by terror and privation, but first of all by a relentless assault on the survivor's sense of purity and worth. Excremental attack, the physical inducement of disgust and self-loathing, was a principal weapon.

But defilement had its lesser logic as well. "In Buchenwald," says one survivor, "it was a principle to depress the morale of prisoners to the lowest possible level, thereby preventing the development of fellow-feeling or co-operation among the victims" (Weinstock, 92). How much self-esteem can one maintain, how readily can one respond with respect to the needs of another, if both stink, if both are caked with mud and feces? We tend to forget how camp prisoners looked and smelled, especially those who had given up the will to live, and in consequence the enormous revulsion and disgust which naturally arose among prisoners. Here was an effective mechanism for intensifying the already heightened irritability of prisoners towards each other, and thus for stifling in common loathing the impulse toward solidarity. Within the camp world all visible signs of human beauty, of bodily pride and spiritual radiance, were thereby to be eliminated from the ranks of the inmates. The prisoner was made to feel subhuman, to see his self-image only in the dirt and stink of his neighbor. The SS, on the contrary, appeared superior not only by virtue of their guns and assurance, but by their elegant apartness from the filth of the prisoner's world. In Auschwitz prisoners were forced to march in the mud, whereas the clean roadway was reserved for the SS.

And here is a final, vastly significant reason why in the camps the prisoners were so degraded. This made it easier for the SS to do their job. It made mass murder less terrible to the murderers, because the victims appeared less than human. They *looked* inferior. In Gitta Sereny's series of interviews with Franz Stangl, commandant of Treblinka, there are moments of fearful insight. Here is one of the most telling:

> *"Why,"* I asked Stangl, *"if they were going to kill them anyway, what was the point of all the humiliation, why the cruelty?"*
>
> "To condition those who actually had to carry out the policies," he said. "To make it possible for them to do what they did" (101).

In a lecture at the New School (New York, 1974), Hannah Arendt remarked that it is easier to kill a dog than a man, easier yet to kill a rat or frog, and no problem at all to kill insects—"It is in the glance, in the eyes." She means that the perception of subjective being in the

victim sparks some degree of identification in the
assailant, and makes his act difficult in proportion to
the capacity for suffering and resistance he perceives.
Inhibited by pity and guilt, the act of murder becomes
harder to perform and results in greater psychic damage to the killer himself. If, on the other hand, the
victim exhibits self-disgust; if he cannot lift his eyes for
humiliation, or if lifted they show only emptiness—
then his death may be administered with ease or even
with the conviction that so much rotten tissue has been
removed from life's body. And it is a fact that in camp
the procedure of "selection"—to the left, life; to the
right, death—was based on physical appearance and on
a certain sense of inward collapse or resilience in the
prospective victim. As a survivor of Auschwitz puts it:

> Yes, here one rotted alive, there was no doubt
> about it, just like the SS in Bitterfield had pre-
> dicted. Yet it was vitally important to keep the
> body clear. . . . Everyone [at a "selection"] had to
> strip and one by one, parade before them naked.
> Mengele in his immaculate white gloves stood point-
> ing his thumb sometimes to the right, sometimes
> to the left. Anyone with spots on the body, or a
> thin *Muselmann*, was directed to the right. That
> side spelt death, the other meant one was allowed
> to rot a little longer (Hart, 65).

With water in permanent shortage; with latrines submerged in their own filth; with diarrhea rife and mud
everywhere, strict cleanliness was just not possible. Simply to *try* to stay clean took extraordinary effort. As
one survivor says: "To pick oneself up, to wash and
clean oneself—all that is the simplest thing in the

world, isn't it? And yet it was not so. Everything in Auschwitz was so organized as to make these things impossible. There was nothing to lean on; there was no place for washing oneself. Nor was there time" (Lewinska, 43). That conditions *were* "so organized" was a dreadful discovery:

> At the outset the living places, the ditches, the mud, the piles of excrement behind the blocks, had appalled me with their horrible filth. . . . And then I saw the light! I saw that it was not a question of disorder or lack of organization but that, on the contrary, a very thoroughly considered conscious idea was in the back of the camp's existence. They had condemned us to die in our own filth, to drown in mud, in our own excrement. They wished to abase us, to destroy our human dignity, to efface every vestige of humanity, to return us to the level of wild animals, to fill us with horror and contempt toward ourselves and our fellows (Lewinska, 41-42).

With this recognition the prisoner either gave up or decided to resist. For many survivors this moment marked the birth of their will to fight back:

> But from the instant when I grasped the motivating principle . . . it was as if I had been awakened from a dream. . . . I felt under orders to live. . . . And if I did die in Auschwitz, it would be as a human being, I would hold on to my dignity. I was not going to become the contemptible, disgusting brute my enemy wished me to be. . . . And a terrible struggle began which went on day and night (Lewinska, 50).

Or as another survivor says:

> There and then I determined that if I did not be-
> come the target of a bullet, or if I were not hanged,
> I would make every effort to endure. No longer
> would I succumb to apathy. My first impulse was
> to concentrate on making myself more presentable.
> Under the circumstances this may sound ludicrous;
> what real relation was there between my new-found
> spiritual resistance and the unsightly rags on my
> body? But in a subtle sense there *was* a relationship,
> and from that moment onwards, throughout my
> life in the camps, I knew this for a fact. I began
> to look around me and saw the beginning of the
> end for any woman who might have had the op-
> portunity to wash and had not done so, or any
> woman who felt that the tying of a shoe-lace was
> wasted energy (Weiss, 84).

Washing, if only in a ritual sense—and quite apart
from reasons of health—was something prisoners
needed to do. They found it necessary to survival, odd
as that may seem, and those who stopped soon died:

> At 4:30, "coffee"—a light mint infusion without
> nourishment and with a repulsive taste—was dis-
> tributed. We often took a few swallows and used
> the rest for washing, but not all of us were able to
> do without this poor substitute for coffee and con-
> sequently many inmates ceased to wash. This was
> the first step to the grave. It was an almost iron
> law: those who failed to wash every day soon
> died. Whether this was the cause or the effect of
> inner breakdown, I don't know; but it was an in-
> fallible symptom (Donat, 173).

Another survivor describes the initial disappearance of concern for his appearance, and the gradual realization that without such care he would not survive:

> Why should I wash? Would I be better off than I am? Would I please someone more? Would I live a day, an hour longer? I would probably live a shorter time, because to wash is an effort, a waste of energy and warmth. . . . But later I understood. . . . In this place it is practically pointless to wash every day in the turbid water of the filthy washbasins for purposes of cleanliness and health; but it is most important as a symptom of remaining vitality, and necessary as an instrument of moral survival (Levi, 35).

By passing through the degradation of the camps, survivors discovered that in extremity a sense of dignity is something which men and women cannot afford to lose. Great damage has to be borne, much humiliation suffered. But at some point a steady resistance to their obliteration as human beings must be made. They learned, furthermore, that when conditions of filth are enforced, befoulment of the body is experienced as befoulment of the soul. And they came to recognize, finally, that when this particular feeling—of something inwardly untouchable—is ruined beyond repair, the will to live dies. To care for one's appearance thus becomes an act of resistance and a necessary moment in the larger structure of survival. Life itself depends on keeping dignity intact, and this, in turn, depends on the daily, never finished battle to remain *visibly* human:

> So we must certainly wash our faces without soap in dirty water and dry ourselves on our jackets.

We must polish our shoes, not because the regulation states it, but for dignity and propriety. We must walk erect, without dragging our feet, not in homage to Prussian discipline but to remain alive, not to begin to die (Levi, 36).

The basic structure of Western civilization or perhaps of any civilization, insofar as the processes of culture and sublimation are one, is the division between body and the spirit, between concrete existence and symbolic modes of being. In extremity, however, divisions like these collapse. The principle of compartmentalization no longer holds, and organic being becomes the immediate locus of selfhood. When this happens, body and spirit become the ground of each other, each bearing the other's need, the other's sorrow, and each responds directly to the other's total condition. If spiritual resilience declines, so does physical endurance. If the body sickens, the spirit too begins to lose its grip. There is a strange circularity about existence in extremity: survivors preserve their dignity in order "not to begin to die"; they care for the body as a matter of "moral survival."

For many among us, the word "dignity" no longer means much; along with terms like "conscience" and "spirit" it has grown suspect and is seldom used in analytic discourse. And certainly, if by "dignity" we mean the projection of pretense and vainglory, or the ways power cloaks itself in pomp and ritual pride; if, that is, we are referring to the parodic forms of this principle, as men exploit it for justification or gain— just as honor and conscience are exploited and likewise parodied, although real in themselves—then of course the claim to dignity is false. But if we mean an inward resistance to determination by external forces; if we are referring to a sense of innocence and worth, something felt to be inviolate, autonomous and untouchable, and which is most vigorous when most threatened; then, as in the survivor's case, we come upon one of the constituents of humanness, one of the irreducible elements of selfhood. Dignity, in this case, appears as a self-conscious, self-determining faculty whose function is to insist upon the recognition of itself *as such*.

Certainly the SS recognized it, and their attempt to destroy it, while not successful in the survivor's case, was one of the worst aspects of the camp ordeal. When cleanliness becomes impossible and human beings are forced to live in their own excretions, their pain becomes intense to the point of agony. The shock of physical defilement causes spiritual concussion, and, simply to judge from the reports of those who have suffered it, subjection to filth seems often to cause greater anguish than hunger or fear of death. "This aspect of our camp life," says one survivor, "was the most dreadful and the most horrible ordeal to which we were subjected" (Weiss, 69). Another survivor describes the plight of men forced to lie in their own excreta: they "moaned and wept with discomfort and disgust. Their moral wretchedness was crushing" (Szalet, 78). In the most bizarre cases, defilement caused a desperation bordering on madness, as when a group of prisoners were forced "to drink out of the toilet bowls":

The men could not bring themselves to obey this devilish order; they only pretended to drink. But the block-fuehrers had reckoned with that; they forced the men's heads deep into the bowls until their faces were covered with excrement. At this the victims almost went out of their minds—that was why their screams had sounded so demented (Szalet, 42).

But why is contact with excrement unbearable? If actual discomfort is minor, why is the reaction so violent? And why does the sense of dignity feel most threatened in this particular case? The incident of the toilet bowls, cited above, has been examined from a psychoanalytic point of view, the conclusion being this:

Infantile satisfactions . . . could be acquired only by means against which culture has erected strong prohibitions. . . . Enforced breakdown of these barriers was capable of bringing the prisoners near to mental disintegration (Bluhm, 15).

The extreme suffering of those men thus resulted from a breach in cultural taboo. Their demented screams issued from the rending of subliminal structures, in response to violation of those "cleanliness habits" which are "enforced by any culture at an early stage of training" (17). The survivor's struggle against an excremental fate, to speak more plainly, is a function of "toilet training"—although that term is not used in the article from which I am quoting, since the degree of reduction it implies, even from a psychoanalytic perspective, seems altogether disproportionate to the violence of the prisoners' experience. The article goes on, however, to suggest that the depth at which the scream originates may reveal, beyond the relative and flexible demands of culture, the violation of a limit or boundary not relative in the same sense:

However, the normal adult of our civilization shares the disgust toward the contact with his excrements with members of tribes who live on the lowest levels of culture. This disgust seems to be a demarkation line, the transgression of which can produce effects much more devastating than the appearance of more or less isolated regressive symptoms (17).

From the psychoanalytic point of view, moral anguish is a product of conflict between cultural demands and the regressive desire to subvert them. But if we keep in mind that all regression is in the service of pleasure, or release from pain (which was Freud's definition of pleasure), then the whole theory of infantile regression, in the survivor's case, becomes absurd. The scream of those desperate men was indeed a defense against dissolution, but to reduce their extraordinary pain to the violation of a taboo, or any restriction merely imposed, seems entirely to miss the point. In any case, the inhibiting authority of toilet training is not so central to selfhood that infraction causes the personality to disintegrate. Only once in Western culture has this been viewed in terms of psychic crisis— among the bourgeois classes in the nineteenth century, with their radical reliance on physical rigidity and, as a consequence, their prurient forms of sexual satisfaction; and I would suggest, finally, that such training is the ritual organization of an inherent biological process. Plenty of taboos went by the board in the concentration camps, but not this one—not, that is, transgression of a "demarkation line" which runs deeper than cultural imposition. What human beings will or will not tolerate depends, up to a point, on training of all kinds. Beyond that, however, there are things absolutely unacceptable because something—let us keep the word

"dignity"—in our deepest nature revolts. And on such
revolt, life in extremity depends.

In *The Symbolism of Evil,* Paul Ricœur defines "dread
of the impure" as the special kind of fear we feel in
reaction to "a threat which, beyond the threat of suffering and death, aims at a diminution of existence, a loss
of the personal core of one's being" (41). That, I think,
is a good description of what survivors feel when threatened by excremental attack. Ricœur goes on to argue
that the feeling of defilement underlies concepts like
"sin" and "guilt," and finally that as "the oldest of the
symbols of evil," defilement "can signify analogically
all the degrees of the experience of evil" (336). And
indeed, why does imagery of washing and physical
purgation underlie our ideas of sanctity and spiritual
purification? Why do we use images associated with
excrement—imagery of corruption and decay, of dirt
and contagion, of things contaminated, rotting or spoiled
—to embody our perceptions of evil? Ricœur concludes
that all such imagery is symbolic only, that it represents
inner states of being—and for us no doubt he is right.
But in the concentration camps, defilement was a condition known by actual sight and touch and smell, and
hence this question: when survivors react so violently
to contact with excrement, are they responding to what
it symbolizes, or is their ordeal the concrete instance
from which our symbolism of evil derives?

The implication of Ricœur's analysis is that "the consciousness of self seems to constitute itself at its lowest
level by means of symbolism and to work out an abstract
language only subsequently" (9). As far as it goes that
is true, yet where does the symbolism originate? How
did defilement come to symbolize evil? Ricœur can only

answer that in the beginning was the symbol—that human selfhood became aware of itself through symbolic objectification of its own structure and condition. This kind of starting point, however, is also a culmination; it is nothing less than the goal of civilization, the outcome of a process of sublimation or transcendence or etherealization (call it what you wish) by which actual events and objects become the images, myths and metaphors that constitute man's spiritual universe. Transformation of the world into symbol is perpetual; thereby we internalize actuality and stay in spiritual, if not in concrete, connection with those primal experiences from which, as civilized beings, we have detached ourselves.

But this activity can be reversed. When civilization breaks down, as it did in the concentration camps, the "symbolic stain" becomes a condition of literal defilement; and evil becomes that which causes real "loss of the personal core of one's being." In extremity man is stripped of his expanded spiritual identity. Only concrete forms of existence remain, actual life and actual death, actual pain and actual defilement; and these now constitute the medium of moral and spiritual being. Spirit does not simply vanish when sublimation fails. At the cost of much of its freedom it falls back to the ground and origin of meaning—back, that is, to the physical experience of the body. Which is another way of saying that, in extremity, symbols tend to actualize.

We might say, then, that in extremity symbolism *as symbolism* loses its autonomy. Or, what amounts to the the same thing, that in this special case everything is felt to be inherently symbolic, intrinsically significant. Either way, meaning no longer exists above and beyond the world; it re-enters concrete experience, becomes immanent and invests each act and moment with urgent depth. And hence the oddly "literary" character of experience in extremity, to which I shall return in Chapter Six. It is as if amid the smoke of burning bodies the great metaphors of world literature were being "acted out" in terrible fact—death and resurrection, damnation and salvation, the whole of spiritual pain and exultation in passage through the soul's dark night.

The following event, for example, seems literary to the point of embarrassment. It is the kind of incident we might expect at the climax of a novel, valid less in itself than as a fiction bearing meaning, and therefore acceptable through the symbolic statement it makes, the psychic drama it embodies. This event, however, happens to be real. It occurred during the last days of the Warsaw Ghetto uprising, it was the fate of many men and women. Armed with handguns and bottles of gasoline, the ghetto fighters held out for fifty-two days against tanks, field artillery and air strikes. So stubbornly did they resist that the Germans finally resorted to burning down the ghetto building by building, street by street, until everything—all life, all sign of man—was gone. The last chance for escape was through the sewers, and down into that foul dark went the remnant of the ghetto:

On the next day, Sunday, April 25, I went down . . . into the underground sewer which led to the "Aryan" side. I will never forget the picture which presented itself to my eyes in the first moment when I descended into the channel. Dozens of refugees . . . sought shelter in these dark and narrow channels awash with filthy water from the municipal latrines and foul refuse flushed down from the private apartments. In these low, narrow channels, only wide enough for one person to crawl forward in a bent position, dozens of people lay jammed and huddled together in the mud and filth (Friedman, 284).

They stayed below, sometimes for days, making their way toward the "free" side, coming up occasionally to see where they were, and then simply waiting. Many died, but through the combined effort of Jewish and Polish partisans, some were rescued and survived:

On May 10, 1943, at nine o'clock in the morning, the lid of the sewer over our heads suddenly opened, and a flood of sunlight streamed into the sewer. At the opening of the sewer Krzaczek [a member of the Polish resistance] was standing and calling all of us to come out, after we had been in the sewer for more than thirty hours. We started to climb out one after another and at once got on a truck. It was a beautiful spring day and the sun warmed us. Our eyes were blinded by the bright light, as we had not seen daylight for many weeks and had spent the time in complete darkness. The streets were crowded with people, and everybody . . . stood still and watched, while strange beings, hardly recognizable as humans, crawled out of the sewers (Friedman, 290).

If that were from a novel, how easily we might speak of rites of passage; of descent into hell; of journey through death's underworld. We would respond to the symbolism of darkness and light, of rebirth and new life, as, blessed by spring and the sun, these slime-covered creatures arise from the bowels of the earth. And we would not be misreading. For despite the horror, it all seems familiar, very much recalling archetypes we know from art and dreams. For the survivor, in any case, the immersion in excrement marks the nadir of his passage through extremity. No worse assault on moral being seems possible. Yet even here there was life and will, as if these shit-smeared bodies were the accurate image of how much mutilation the human spirit can bear, despite shame, loathing, the trauma of violent recoil, and still keep the sense of something inwardly inviolate. "Only our feverish eyes," said one survivor of the sewers, "still showed that we were living human beings" (Friedman, 289).

IV

NIGHTMARE AND WAKING

Whenever I recall the first days at the camp, I still grow hot and cold with nameless terror. . . . Three weeks after I arrived at Auschwitz, I still could not believe it. I lived as in a dream, waiting for someone to awaken me.

OLGA LENGYEL
Five Chimneys

It seemed almost a luxury to die, to go to sleep and never wake up again.

GERDA KLEIN
All But My Life

ONE SURVIVOR remarks that in camp he did not wake fellow prisoners when one of them was having a nightmare; he knew that no matter how bad the dream might be, reality was worse. And what, really, could be worse than to wake up in a concentration camp? "The most ghastly moment of the twenty-four hours of camp life," says a survivor of Auschwitz, "was the awakening, when, at a still nocturnal hour, the three shrill blows of a whistle tore us pitilessly from our exhausted sleep and from the longings of our dreams" (Frankl, 31). "The moment of awakening," says another, "was the most horrible" (Zywulska, 33). Or finally:

Awakening is the hardest moment—no matter whether these are your first days in the camp, days full of despair, where every morning you relive the painful shock, or whether you have been here long, very long, where each morning reminds you that you lack strength to begin a new day, a day identical with all previous days (Szmaglewska, 4).

The wonder is they got up at all. Camp prisoners were permanently exhausted, they were often sick, and a night's sleep was four or five hours at most. Under such stress we might expect a retreat into unconsciousness, into coma, as when a person faints from shock or excess of pain. Where did the strength to get up come from? And why return to a reality so terrible? Prisoners were driven awake by fear, by anxiety, and often by the blows of a whip or club. But mainly they got up for the same reason any of us do: essential activities have to be performed; organisms must interact with, and find protection from, their environment. Prisoners either got up or died; they either faced an unbearable world knowing they would have to bear it, or gave up.

The whole of the survivor's fate is in that moment. It was always a battle in itself, but it was also part of a larger fight, not just against weakness and despair, but finally against sleep itself because sleep was dangerous. There was never time for sufficient rest, and this elementary need thus became a constant temptation, enforced by extreme exhaustion but even more by the yearning to quit, to sink into the blank peace of oblivion and stay there. Many prisoners were shot or beaten to death for crawling off to some corner and falling asleep. Many others froze to death while sleeping in the snow. At any moment of relaxed striving, sleep could become a part of the slide toward death, a surrender of the will to shove on. "There was absolutely no relaxation possible at Auschwitz" (Kessel, 106). Or again, "The only escape is in sleep, but sleep means death" (Ekart, 46).

The fact that prisoners remained sane with so little rest and under such pressure argues a radical revision of the body's basic rhythms and therefore an agency beyond will alone. Sleep and waking are phases in a process biologically determined, and we may speculate that in extremity men and women find a foundation for struggle in the organic activities of daily life, as if these were indeed *acts of life*. Every morning the survivor's will had to be renewed, and it was: not through some secret fortitude of the heart, but through the physical act of getting up. The pain might be enormous, despair complete, but the commitment—to that day, to that much more of existence—was made. A survivor of Auschwitz describes it this way: "I climb down on to the floor and put on my shoes. The sores on my feet reopen at once, and a new day begins" (Levi, 57).

When the camp experience is viewed as a whole, a remarkable parallel appears between each morning's waking and a larger aspect of the survivor's ordeal. The first encounter with extremity immersed prisoners in a world of pure terror, a world in which nothing made sense or promised hope. The impact was so sudden and overwhelming that the self floundered and began to disintegrate. In shock and disbelief, prisoners went about as if asleep, as if locked in a horrid dream, not responding intelligently, not looking out for themselves. The first phase of survival experience may thus be described as a period of *initial collapse*. Given time, however, breakdown was followed by a second stage, characterized by reintegration and recovery of stable selfhood. Very much as if they were waking up, survivors went from withdrawal to engagement, from passivity to resistance. They emerged from their dream-state to face what had to be faced.

Coming from our world, with no prior knowledge of extremity, new prisoners were in no way prepared for the frenzy of their first days in camp. Here is what it was like—after days in a cattle-car without water or room for rest, standing in excrement and vomit—to arrive:

The wagon doors were torn ajar. The shouts were deafening. S.S. men with whips and half-wild Alsatian dogs swarmed all over the place. Uncontrolled fear brought panic as families were ruthlessly torn apart. Parents screamed for lost children and mothers shrieked their names over the voices of the bawling guards. Everyone without exception lost both nerves and senses (Unsdorfer, 72).

It was an onslaught not to be withstood. When the train doors opened, prisoners were faced with an incomprehensible world: beating and shooting; families dispersed; and those not "selected" for immediate extermination driven into crowded buildings where everything—possessions, clothes, hair, name—was stripped from them. The magnitude and speed of these events made sane response impossible. What kind of sense, after all, was the incoming prisoner to make of his or her first march through Auschwitz:

Corpses were strewn all over the road; bodies were hanging from the barbed-wire fence; the sound of shots rang in the air continuously. Blazing flames shot into the sky; a giant smoke cloud ascended above them. Starving, emaciated human skeletons stumbled toward us, uttering incoherent sounds. They fell down right in front of our eyes, and lay there gasping out their last breath (Newman, 18).

The otherness of the camps, their horror and apparent chaos, was not real by past standards; unable to root itself in familiar ground, the old self fell apart. A similar disintegration was suffered by Soviet prisoners who, as soon as they were arrested, were subjected to a

process which would not end until the prisoner broke
down and signed a false confession:

> Interrogations by night and special cells ensure that
> the prisoner is not allowed to sleep for one mo-
> ment. After five to eight days without sleep he is
> subject to increasingly severe hallucinations and
> these can be further intensified by blows. The
> prisoner loses his self-control. His personality be-
> gins to split, to dissolve and to be transformed. . . .
> He loses the power to distinguish between reality
> and possibility. He loses touch with himself. All
> that remains of him is a twitching point of ref-
> erence between vague terror without an object,
> the pervasive feeling of imposed guilt and confus-
> ing hallucinations (Roeder, 11).

There are heroic accounts of resistance to that kind
of treatment, especially Arthur London's *The Confession* and Alexander Weissberg's *The Accused*. London
broke down in the end, and even Weissberg, whose endurance seems superhuman, went through brief periods
of collapse:

> It had now been made clear that the examiner was
> not interested in the truth and wanted fictitious
> self-accusations. If that were the case then I was
> really lost. . . . This feeling of being hopelessly
> trapped paralysed me. . . . So far I had confessed
> nothing, but I felt now that my reason was about
> to break down (Weissberg, 219).

Or as an American survivor of the Soviet camps told
me: "Oh yes, after enough beating at the base of the
spine, after enough kicks in the genitals, you would sign

anything." To sign was to say to them and to yourself that you were not who you had been. Temporarily, the old self dissolved. And for Soviet and Nazi prisoners alike, this first stage was decisive:

> Every new-comer immediately had to traverse a course of profound personal degradation and humiliation. Naked he was driven through the unbridgeable abyss that separated the two worlds, "outside" and "inside." It was the immediate effects of this terrifying act of compulsion that determined the ultimate destiny of a prisoner. There were two possibilities and within three months it became apparent which one would apply. By that time a man would have gone into an almost irresistible mental decline—if, indeed, he had not already perished in a physical sense; or he would have begun to adapt himself to the concentration camp (Kogon, 274).

In *The Informed Heart* Bruno Bettelheim observes that the "vast majority of the thousands of prisoners who died at Buchenwald each year died soon" (146). That was true everywhere in the world of the camps: newcomers had the highest death rate. We might therefore ask, as Bettelheim does, "why, in the concentration camp, although some prisoners survived and others got killed, such a sizable number simply died" (145). His answer is that they "died of exhaustion, both physical and psychological, due to a loss of desire to live" (146). Loss of desire to live is one of the primary symptoms of the period of initial collapse, and large numbers of men and women died because during this crucial stage of imprisonment they failed to strive for life with every fiber of their being. But still, loss of the will to live is a symptom, not a cause. The fact is that prisoners "died soon" from a complex of conditions and forces which nothing in the whole of their lives had prepared them to face or even imagine: from prolonged terror and shock; from radical loss, both of identity and of faith in the capacity of goodness to prevail against the evil surrounding them. They died simply for lack of information, because they did not know what to do or how to act. Very often, too, they died of mourning, of grief for the deaths of their family and friends. As one survivor remembers of the time when her friends were killed: "That day I no longer wanted to fight for my life" (Hart, 81). And when the death of one's children or parents or spouse or all of these at once was involved, the state of mourning—of the desire to rejoin those whose death is experienced as a death in the self —could last months, a time during which the mourner was especially vulnerable.

Here, in fact, is the deepest cause of early death: the horror and irreparable hurt felt by the prisoner when he or she first encounters the spectacle of atrocity. Moral disgust, if it arises too abruptly or becomes too intense, expresses itself in the desire to die, to have done with such a world. Perhaps to some small degree we feel this ourselves, a little more each evening as news of the day's evil—the massacres, the mass starvations, the betrayals of leadership—batters away at our faith in human virtue. How much more compelling for those actually *there,* suddenly a part of the worst world possible. For them there comes a point after which no feeling remains except absolute refusal to go on existing when existence itself seems vile beyond redemption. One survivor, having experienced this feeling herself, includes in her testimony a letter from a friend who died. I quote it at length, asking the reader to ignore the pathos in order to understand without special sentiment how "loss of desire to live" comes about:

Do you know what happened? No, you don't know. Yesterday, yes, it was yesterday, early in the morning we heard a lot of noise—screams and crying and begging for mercy. . . . Quickly my father and I ran down the back stairs to hide in the basement, while Mother went to get the baby. . . . We heard distant screams for hours and hours. Only when night fell was it quiet. We hoped and prayed that Mama and the child had found refuge somewhere. After it had been dark for hours we crawled out of the cellar. . . . We went to the street. We went to all the homes. We met a few ghostlike people who were swaying as if coming from another world. . . . Finally, we met a young man who told us the tragic tale. Old people, young people, and children all had been taken to the market place. There they had undressed and lain naked on the stones, face down, and the murderers on horses and brandishing guns trampled on that screaming human pavement. . . . those who remained alive had to march naked outside the town. They had to dig their own grave and stand on the rim until a hail of bullets killed them. . . . We went there. . . . We saw a great square grave, half-open yet, a mountain of naked bodies in it. Many we recognized. We found my mother. She was all bloody. We did not find my little brother. I found Henek, the one I loved more than life, who was to be my husband. . . . Not one tear did I shed in that grave. Only my heart died. Do you know what? If they would come tomorrow and kill my father I would not care. I would not cry. I would be glad

for him. I wish they would kill me. From now on
I will walk wherever it is not permitted. I want
them to catch me. I want them to kill me because
I don't care (Klein, 69-70) .

For that girl one question was left: "Why does the
world go on when things like this happen?" Every survivor must face this question. It bothers us too, now
and then, except that for us despair is not fatal. Life
goes on, if only through routine and habit. For all those
who "died soon," however, the initial immersion in horror was like a well of sorrow to which there is no bottom. Survivors are proof that the desire to live returns.
It returns, but slowly, through an inner process of
regeneration which takes time. Vast numbers of men
and women died because they did not have time, the
blessing of sheer time, to recover. Something—typhus,
starvation, an SS bullet—killed them before they regained their will to live. As a survivor of Buchenwald
says: "It took a long time for a mind, torn from the
anchorages of the outside world and thrust into life-
and-death turmoil, to find a new inward center of grav-
ity" (Kogon, 276).

Speaking of his own camp experience, Bettelheim observes that "right from the beginning I became convinced that these dreadful and degrading experiences
were somehow not happening to 'me' as a subject, but
only to 'me' as object" (127). Elie Cohen, another
psychiatrist who survived the camps, calls this the
"stage of initial reaction"; he too emphasizes the "sub-
ject-object split," and identifies it by describing his own
response to atrocity: "My reaction to this, I observed,
was an apparent splitting of my personality. I felt as if

I did not belong, as if the business did not concern me" (116). Viktor Frankl, a third psychiatrist to pass through the camps, divides the period of initial collapse into two stages: first shock, then apathy. The new prisoner undergoes "a kind of emotional death" (18), which Frankl sees as a "necessary mechanism of self-defense" (27). Cohen, however, points out that although apathy keeps madness and despair at a distance, it produces a dangerous disregard for the environment:

> In my opinion the after-effect of the fright reaction in most prisoners was followed by the phase of apathy, which for many was a period fraught with extreme danger. As they took no interest in their surroundings and did not strive after self-preservation, reacting tardily and behaving as if they had been "sandbagged," their behavior was not such as is best suited to a concentration camp. The duration of this fright apathy is limited; I would estimate it at no more than one or two weeks. But after this the prisoner was not yet in a condition to make an attempt at adaptation, for with the dwindling of his apathy, mourning made itself felt to its fullest extent, and the mournfully depressive phase set in. . . . For very many prisoners [this] period proved too long, so that they never had an opportunity to engage in the struggle for adaptation (169).

That is the experience of initial collapse in clinical terms. The majority of survivors, however, do not use technical language. For them, entry into the camp world was characterized by an overriding sense of *nightmare* and *unreality*—two words which appear constantly when survivors refer to their first days and weeks:

> All around us were screams, death, smoking chim-
> neys making the air black and heavy with soot and
> the smell of burning bodies. . . . It was just like a
> nightmare and it took weeks and weeks before I
> could really believe this was happening (Hart,
> 92-93).

But unlike our use of such words (to inject a little drama into ordinary life), survivors speak this way because by any standard of communicable perception or past experience, the first weeks in camp were literally unreal and embedded in nightmare. "Not only during the transport," says Bettelheim, "but for a long time to come, prisoners had to convince themselves that this was real and not just a nightmare" (127).

To the extent that "reality" is a cultural construct, then of course the camps were unreal. At least in Western Europe there had been two centuries of steady advance in political and economic well-being, with much praise of "Progress" and "Humanity," on the assumption that these providential agencies were fully capable of taking a lost God's place. The homeland of Kant and Goethe was renowned for its *Kultur,* for its *Geistesbildung,* and in Russia the new age of justice had arrived. Man was emerging from the dark past of his childhood. Imbued with such preponderant "faith in humanity," how indeed were the victims to believe, let alone make sense of, the inhumanity massing to destroy them? Evil on such a scale was not believable. As one survivor says, "We fell victim to our faith in mankind, our belief that humanity had set limits to the degradation and persecution of one's fellow man" (Donat, 103).

Or as another survivor puts it, this time in direct answer to our questions:

> Why? Why did we walk like meek sheep to the slaughter-house? Why did we not fight back? . . . I know why. Because we had faith in humanity. Because we did not really think that human beings were capable of committing such crimes (Klein, 89).

The concentration camps were *in* this world and yet *not* in this world, places where behavior was grossly exaggerated, without apparent logic, yet fiercely hostile and encompassing. These are the components of nightmare, and if they join with the prisoner's psychic state —the confusion and stunned emotion, the dread and impotence, the split between a self that is victim and a self which, as through the wrong end of a telescope, merely watches—then the sense of nightmare is bound to prevail. During this time the prisoner suffers a terrible sleep, as when the young Wiesel saw what in shape and feeling could only be a nightmare:

> Not far from us, flames were leaping up from a ditch, gigantic flames. They were burning something. A lorry drew up at the pit and delivered its load—little children. Babies! Yes, I saw it—saw it with my own eyes. . . . Was I awake? I could not believe it. . . . No, none of this could be true. It was a nightmare (*Night*, 42).

Wiesel is not being literary, he is not using metaphor to enforce his perceptions. He is making the only reference remotely adequate to what he saw and felt. The dream of Hell, which for millennia had haunted Western consciousness, was now actual. Prisoners found themselves *in* it; just as we might find ourselves in a bad dream, without sense or perspective or relation. And as with nightmare, one tries to escape: either by saying that it is "only a dream," or by striving to "wake up."

But it was deadly to remain within the dream. Prisoners unable to shake off their sense of unreality could only drift as one drifts in dream, defenseless and stupid. Viktor Frankl observes that to regard camp existence as "unreal was in itself an important factor in causing the prisoners to lose their hold on life" (71). The alternative was to wake up, to replace apathy with struggle and transcend the derangement of nightmare by recovering moral perspective:

> Many times I felt I must be dreaming, and I would call to myself: "Wake up! Wake up! You are having a nightmare!" I would look around me, trying to wake up, but alas, my eyes kept on seeing the same dismal picture. Finally, I would start to shake all over, and I would say to myself: "You are in a concentration camp, in an annihilation camp. Don't let them get you down." I didn't want to end up in the furnace; I wanted to live to tell of this (Newman, 20).

This survivor of Auschwitz would "call" to herself as if split into distant selves, the one passive, the other helpless but aware of the need to act. The dream is not a dream, there is no way out, and once she begins to admit the truth of her predicament the sense of unreality fades. By coming to face the evil of the world she is in, she gains a perspective which sets her apart. Selfhood, realism, and the desire to live emerge together ("I didn't want to end up in the furnace") and culminate in the will to bear witness ("I wanted to live to tell of this").

The survivor turns back to life because a process of healing, of inner repair, has had the time to complete itself. The mind grows able to respond once more, and here a final factor is evident, for very often the moment of waking occurred in response to a specifically human act or circumstance. In the following instance a survivor of Maidanek and Auschwitz describes her breakdown and the care of a friend which gave her the time and encouragement to recover:

> The shock that followed the unexpected loss of my mother, my frantic terror at the sight of the watch-towers, the machine-guns . . . drove me almost to the point of insanity. . . . and at a time when I should have forced myself to be as resistant as possible, I broke down completely. . . . Meanwhile Hela fought with redoubled strength—for herself and for me. She shared every bite she acquired with me. . . . Had it not been for Hela's efforts, I would not have roused myself from my apathy and despair (Birenbaum, 94-96).

Suicide, or rather its failure, was also effective. It shocked the prisoner back to life as if—and this may actually apply to all survivors who come through the period of collapse—the will to survive were born by subjectively passing through death. I have talked about this with survivors, and their stories are repeated in the case of a Soviet prisoner who attempted to hang himself. With the return to consciousness came a feeling of intense decision:

During the following 17 years I was to go through unbelievable trials, trials in which death would have come as a real balm, but I never thought for a second to try it again. From that one wretched moment I was determined to survive (Solomon, 16).

Sometimes the catalyst was shock, sometimes the slow penetration of care. Often it was a new-found purpose—as when a survivor of Maidanek began "card-filing" the incoming prisoners:

I thought of my arrival and my first impressions of the camp. I knew that a person coming to a camp was afraid of everything and everybody, that she was distracted and terrified. The first word was so important. I decided to be patient, to answer all questions, to calm them and give them courage. My life began to hold meaning (Zywulska, 113).

Typically also, the moment of waking coincided with the resolution to bear witness or with the decision to resist defilement. And often, too, survivors were jarred back to life by the same horror that, earlier, had paralyzed them. During one survivor's first days "there were moments when I could scarcely resist the temptation to end my life"; but one morning when he saw how the guards "piled up the dead bodies like steps of stairs, how the blockfuehrers played football with them, I put from me all thought of suicide" (Szalet, 52). Another survivor, a doctor, accidentally witnessed the end of a group of pregnant women and came to see that against such evil the alternative to death is revolt:

They were beaten with clubs and whips, torn by dogs, dragged around by the hair and kicked in the stomach. . . . Then, when they collapsed, they were thrown into the crematory—alive. I stood, rooted to the ground, unable to move, to scream, to run away. But gradually the horror turned into revolt and this revolt shook me out of my lethargy and gave me a new incentive to live. I had to remain alive. . . . It was up to me to save the life of the mothers, if there was no other way, then by destroying the life of their unborn children (Peri, 80-81).

That kind of decision—to save life through death—was forced upon survivors repeatedly, and I shall return to it in Chapter Five. The point now is that like each morning's waking, these moments of return to the world are psychic acts of *turning,* from passivity to action, from horror to the daily business of staying alive—as if one turned one's actual gaze from left to right, from darkness to possible light. As one survivor says, "I simply did not dwell on the horrors I was living through" (Donat, 304). There was no other way, and to become a survivor, every inmate had to make this turn. Once it was made the possibility of coming through was greatly increased, for now some part, at least, of their fate was up to them. They now paid sharp attention, not to the horror or to their own pain, but to the development of objective conditions which had to be judged constantly in terms of their potential for life or for death. Survivors thus acquire a capacity for realism, impersonal and without the least illusion, a realism which one survivor has called "the inhuman frankness of Auschwitz," and with it the ability to learn, to know, to fight back in small ways:

The longer we stayed in the camp, the more we gained in experience, our instincts sharpened, our vigilance developed and our reactions quickened. We acquired a greater capacity for adapting ourselves to conditions (Birenbaum, 103).

They turned to face the worst straight-on, without sentiment or special hope, simply to keep watch over life. And when the moment of turning came, finally, it was attended by a strong sensation of choice, a feeling of new determination, as if the decision to survive were an inner fate expressing itself through a conscious assent of the will. As one survivor says, "It was then, faced with this spectacle of physical decay, with death rising like a tide on all sides, that I decided in my mind that I must live" (Bernard, 87). That is the moment of waking, of return; and this book, as I write, enacts the same resolution, the same kind of turn—away from the monstrous inhumanity of the concentration camps, away from the despair and nihilism they authorize, back to the small strands of life and decency which constitute, however faint and scattered, a fabric of discernible goodness amid that evil.

But for many the turn never came. For them there was neither luck nor time. These people, thousands of them, were called the *Muselmänner,* the "moslems" or "walking dead," for whom time ran out before they were able to shake the sense of nightmare and wake to their predicament. They starved, they fell sick, they stumbled into situations which got them killed. For them the collapse was too much, too many psychic and physical blows too fast, until the momentum of decline increased beyond reversal. They died inwardly, and as their spirit withered their outward aspect was terrible to see:

> They behaved as if they were not thinking, not feeling, unable to act or respond. . . . Typically, this stopping of action began when they no longer lifted their legs as they walked, but only shuffled them. When finally even the looking about on their own stopped, they soon died (Bettelheim, 152-53).

This is the empirical instance of death-in-life. No more awful thing can be said of the concentration camps than that countless men and women were murdered in spirit as the means of killing them in body. Primo Levi has suggested that if we were to pull all the evil of our age into one image, it would be this face with dead eyes. In Levi's description we get some idea of the logical fate, the fate most feared, most nearly suffered, by everyone who passed through the camps:

> On their entry into the camp, through basic incapacity, or by misfortune, or through some banal incident, they are overcome before they can adapt themselves; they are beaten by time, they do not begin to learn German, to disentangle the infernal knot of laws and prohibitions until their body is already in decay, and nothing can save them from selections or from death by exhaustion. Their life is short, but their number is endless; they, the *Muselmänner,* the drowned, form the backbone of the camp, an anonymous mass, continually renewed and always identical, of non-men who march and labour in silence, the divine spark dead within them, already too empty to really suffer. One hesi-

tates to call them living; one hesitates to call their
death death (82).

To say "they went to their death like sheep" is easy
enough, and we say it often indeed. Thereby our own
fear finds expression, our own terror and doubt to be
concealed even as we imply that we know better than
they what it must be like to wake up in a concentration
camp, to carry on through nightmare, to turn back somehow to that world. Whatever our reasons, we can make
such assumptions only by disregarding a cardinal fact
about the survivor's experience: *all things human take
time,* time which the damned never have, time for life
to repair at least the worst of its wounds. It took time
to wake, time for horror to incite revolt, time for the
recovery of lucidity and will. Imagine the time necessary
to carry through a major resistance action in a concentration camp—the infinitely slow work of regenerating
will and self-respect, of building trust, of making contacts, getting arms, sustaining deaths and betrayals,
establishing accurate plans and then, together, moving
as they did in Buchenwald, in Auschwitz, Sobibor, Treblinka. Everything depended on time, and in the interim
chance ruled supreme. Any accumulation of too much
bad luck at once—to be exhausted and starving and
then get sick and *then* be savagely beaten—and the frail
spirit broke. This happened most often to new prisoners;
but it could happen to anyone, and the survivor's greatest fear was that through a run of bad luck he or she
would sink irreversibly into the masses of the doomed.

In almost all accounts by survivors the spectacle of
these truly "dead souls" is mentioned, and always with
the same mixture of pity and revulsion. In the Soviet
camps they were called *dokhodyaga,* the "goners," and

the fear they inspire arises from the *visible* process of
spirit in decay:

There was a man squatting on a rubbish heap. He
must have broken down—mentally, I mean, and
that was the end, physically too, in every case—
and if he found a fish head, he tried to suck the
eyes and did things like that (Knapp, 77).

That, for survivors, was worse than being killed outright. And it was always possible, for once the will to
live had been regained it was constantly undermined by
chance and despair. Prisoners survived by chance, they
died by chance, and they *knew* it. In one instance a
group of women were rounded up at random and locked
in the gas chamber. All night they stood jammed against
each other waiting; at dawn they were released because
the SS had run out of gas, and by the time the next supply arrived it was someone else's turn. And always,
around that corner, around this one, there might be an
SS man drunk and killing for the fun of it: "Their hands
were never far from their revolvers and even without
provocation they would draw them and shoot a prisoner
in the face at close range" (Vrba, 209). It was indeed
hopeless, and yet the alternative was either to quit and
join the *Muselmänner*, or to strive anyway, *as if* chance
were to some extent on one's side. A survivor of Birkenau put it this way: "She knows that a number of circumstances evoked by orders or accidents may cause her
annihilation, but she knows too that there is a chance
to escape death and that it is up to her to win the
game" (Szmaglewska, 117).

But still it was hopeless. The striking fact is that from
a logical point of view, resistance and survival were
just not possible. The following dialogue, between two

women in Auschwitz, expressed the general outlook among survivors:

> "There's no hope for us."
> And her hand makes a gesture and the gesture evokes rising smoke.
> "We must fight with all our strength."
> "Why? . . . Why fight since all of us have to . . ."
> The hand completes the gesture. Rising smoke.
> "No. We must fight."
> "How can we hope to get out of here. How could anyone ever get out of here. It would be better to throw ourselves on the barbed wire right now."
> What is there to say to her. She is small, sickly. And I am unable to persuade myself. All arguments are senseless. I am at odds with my reason. One is at odds with all reason (Delbo, 18).

The survivor's will to go on is illogical, irrational, stupid with another wisdom. Just to *read* descriptions of camp conditions leads to loss of faith in the prospect of survival. Life seems so clearly impossible against such odds. Yet in extremity the function of intelligence is not to judge one's chances, which are nearly zero, but to make the most of each day's opportunity for getting through *that* day: "I realized, after what I had seen, that my attitude to Auschwitz would have to change. No longer was it simply a question of surviving. It was a question of surviving today without thinking too much about tomorrow" (Vrba, 108). At any moment the survivor might be killed, might be hurt badly enough in mind and body to make *another* return impossible. But until then, he or she hangs on despite evidence on all sides that death is inevitable. As long as the spirit does not break, the survivor keeps mute faith in life. Against the knowledge of chance and hopelessness there is another, more intimate knowledge—an awareness of "that puzzling potential of inner strength," as one survivor says,

> . . . which permits your body to keep warm though the penetrating chill freezes the soil and clots the damp sand, which permits you to keep the cheerfulness of spirit though death and extermination are all about you, which permits you to have faith that the Germans will lose though you are surrounded—take that railroad track, for instance, with its purposeful shipment—by evidences of their power (Szmaglewska, 125).

Life in extremity reveals in its movement a definite rhythm of decline and renewal. The state of wakefulness is essential, but in actual experience it is less an unwavering hardness of spirit than a tenuous achievement with periods of weakness and strength. Survivors not only wake, but reawake, fall low and begin to die, and then turn back to life. This happened to individual inmates all the time. Sometimes just the shock of realizing that one was becoming a *Muselman* was enough to inspire new will. But often, too, the experience of renewal was shared, sometimes in moments of intense solidarity:

> Pain and . . . fear . . . kept us awake. A cloudless sky, thickly set with glittering stars, looked in upon our grief-filled prison. The moon shone through the window. Its light was dazzling that night and gave the pale, wasted faces of the prison-

ers a ghostly appearance. It was as if all the life had ebbed out of them. I shuddered with dread, for it suddenly occurred to me that I was the only living man among corpses.

All at once the oppressive silence was broken by a mournful tune. It was the plaintive tones of the ancient "Kol Nidre" prayer. I raised myself up to see whence it came. There, close to the wall, the moonlight caught the uplifted face of an old man, who, in self-forgetful, pious absorption, was singing softly to himself. . . . His prayer brought the ghostly group of seemingly insensible human beings back to life. Little by little, they all roused themselves and all eyes were fixed on the moonlight-flooded face.

We sat up very quietly, so as not to disturb the old man, and he did not notice that we were listening. . . . When at last he was silent, there was exaltation among us, an exaltation which men can experience only when they have fallen as low as we had fallen and then, through the mystic power of a deathless prayer, have awakened once more to the world of the spirit (Szalet, 70-71).

On its collective level, this movement away from, and then back toward, life and humanness was more apparent in the Soviet camps, where the impact of some rumor or special event would cause the mood of the entire camp to rise or fall. In the following instance a kind of general resurrection occurred when everyone in camp was allowed a "free" day, with no work and maybe a bit of extra food:

At every step, in every corner of the barrack, the approaching holiday could be sensed. I could never understand how so much politeness suddenly appeared from under the shell of indifference and mutual hatred. As they talked, the men showed each other so much courtesy and friendliness that, looking at them, I could almost forget that I was in prison. There was a stench of bad breath and sweat in the barrack, clouds of steam seeped in from the door and the faces seemed to blur in the murky light, but despite all this there was so much life and happy excitement there, so much hope and feeling. . . . Good-night, good-night, excited voices whispered all around, sleep well, tomorrow is our holiday, tomorrow is a day of rest (Herling, 116).

And sometimes, finally, this kind of rebirth came with all the pain and mystery of actual birth, as if the two were but different instances of an identical process. To go into a camp "hospital" was not to expect improvement, since the main function of such places was to gather up the dead and dying. There was little treatment, often none at all, and here the diseases of the camp were assembled without precaution. In the Nazi camps, the worst cases were regularly "selected" for extermination, and terrible "experiments" were performed. A prisoner went into the camp hospital fairly sure that life was finished. The temptation to quit was very strong, and yet in these places too, many men and women regained the desire to live. And as experienced, it felt as if the power of life itself were pulling them back to the world:

The first thing the dying woman feels upon return to consciousness is pain. She is not yet fully awake after her exhausting delirium and she already feels a pain deep within her, near the heart, just as if a kind hand lovingly hugged the heart, forgetting that this may hurt. . . . When the body lies shrunken to a childish form, when arms and legs have become like thin twigs, when the mouth is parched and puckered, when every bite of food causes the return of dysentery, when the very smell of the camp soup brings on nausea, when there is no help, no care, no medicine—whence comes this magic will to live? Where is it born, in which recess of the human body does it bud and blossom so strongly that it can conquer Death in his many shapes? Whence comes that imperishable will power to find the means of defense? (Szmaglewska, 49).

These are the questions, addressed not to the fact that so many died, but to the fact that some survived. And the answers can only lie in life itself. There is a power at the center of our being, at the heart of all things living. But only in man does it assume a spiritual character. And only through spirit does life continue by decision. "Human beings are like weeds," said a Soviet prisoner to his cellmates. "They take some killing. Now if you treated horses like this they'd be dead in a couple of days" (Weissberg, 389). But this answer only points to a deeper question. Perhaps we shall not fathom the wonder of life at its roots, or discern how strength can rest on such frail foundations. Only within the last hundred years have the biological sciences begun to formulate objectively what might be meant by "life in itself." I shall return to this in Chapter Seven, but already we can grasp some part, at least, of what the survivor's experience reveals: that whether felt as a power, or observed as a system of activities, life is existence laboring to sustain itself, repairing, defending, healing.

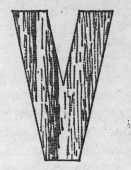

LIFE IN DEATH

In my happier days I used to remark on the aptitude of the saying, "When in life we are in the midst of death." I have since learnt that it's more apt to say, "When in death we are in the midst of life."

A BELSEN SURVIVOR

In our group we shared everything; and the moment one of the group ate something without sharing it, we knew it was the beginning of the end for him.

A TREBLINKA SURVIVOR

IN *NIGHT,* Elie Wiesel records two moments of advice, two prescriptions for survival in the concentration camps. The first came from an "old" prisoner speaking to the new arrivals:

> We are all brothers, and we are all suffering the same fate. The same smoke floats over all our heads. Help one another. It is the only way to survive (52).

The second was an anonymous inmate's comment:

> Listen to me, boy. Don't forget that you're in a concentration camp. Here, every man has to fight for himself and not think of anyone else. Even of his father. Here, there are no fathers, no brothers, no friends. Everyone lives and dies for himself alone (122).

Help one another. Every man for himself. The conflict is classic, and nowhere more starkly stressed than in the concentration-camp ordeal. For as soon as survivors wake to the reality of their predicament they must choose. They must decide which view will govern their behavior and their perception of camp life as a whole. In extremity the claims of self-interest seem sounder, more logical; and the second prescription—help only thyself—dominates the description of events in Wiesel's books: men fight among themselves, fathers contend with sons to the death. The rule of war was total, or so he implies. Yet Wiesel did not abandon his father, and the prisoner who gave kind advice was, after all, a man living in Auschwitz.

There is a contradiction in Wiesel's view of the camps, a contradiction which occurs so often in reports by survivors that it amounts to a double vision at the heart of their testimony. In *The Holocaust Kingdom,* Alexander Donat describes Maidanek as a world in which "the doomed devoured each other," but he includes another kind of evidence as well, for instance his near death from a beating he received for refusing to beat others, and the help he was given, when he was desperately in need of time to recover, by someone who found him a clerking job. Likewise, in his account of survival in Auschwitz, Sim Kessel says: "Intelligence, courage, knowledge, vitality, the desire to live—all counted for nothing. . . . common misery reduced everyone to the same level, erasing all values, breaking down all wills" (10). He sticks to this assessment, despite examples of courage and quick-wittedness, despite his own slow coming to terms with the knowledge of how to survive. He says all concern for others vanished; yet one morning when, like countless others, Kessel collapsed in the snow and could not get up, "two neighbors leaned over me, saying that I was feverish and they would help me. And so they did; they supported me, almost carrying me at times" (161). They never knew his name, nor he theirs.

Acts of care and decency seem so out of place in the camps that survivors themselves are perplexed. In his description of the Soviet camps, Jerzy Gliksman states that "the conditions in which we had to live aroused the worst instincts in all of us. All trace of human solidarity vanished" (217). But here again the principle of jungle rule is belied by events which Gliksman describes in the course of his story. Most striking, perhaps, is the moment when night-blindness (a frequent illness among vitamin-starved prisoners in the northern camps) made his predicament "most desperate":

> One evening as I was walking . . . with my arms stretched out in front of me, like a real blind man, an unknown individual took me by the arm and conducted me to a spot that had more light. . . . "Don't you recognize me? . . . I am Berg . . . don't you remember me from Kotlas?" (301).

Kotlas was the transit camp where they had met and briefly talked. Berg knew his way around better and was able to get a job for Gliksman in one of the innumerable GULAG file rooms, with an improvement in shelter and light which saved his life. Gliksman concludes the episode by saying: "To the present day I do not know why this man, almost a total stranger, did me such a good turn" (304).

Incidents like these seem exceptional, as indeed they were, and yet they happened all the time—a fact which does not negate the savagery of existence in the camps, but which qualifies the view of "all against all" and needs accounting for. Reports by survivors regularly include small deeds of courage and resistance, of help and mutual care; but in the larger picture, the image of viciousness and death grows to such enormous intensity that all else—any sign of elementary humanness—pales to insignificance. And surely this is understandable. The element of chance was so pervasive, the moments of salvation so unexpected, that the power of human encounters seemed slight and difficult to make sense of. Shock was another factor; what impressed survivors most indelibly was death, suffering, terror, all on a scale of magnitude and monstrosity not to be faced without lasting trauma. Primarily, however, survivors stress the negative side of camp existence because their accounts are governed by an obsessive need to "tell the world" of the terrible things they have seen. This determines not only the kind of material they select to record, but also the emphasis they give it. As a witness, the survivor aims above all to convey the otherness of the camps, their specific inhumanity.

But the contradiction goes deeper than that. The essential paradox of extremity is that life persists in a world ruled by death. Life-in-death characterizes every aspect of the survivor's experience, for in order to live and stay human, the survivor must be in the world but not of it. That, of course, is an old distinction. For the Stoic or the Christian it was mainly a matter of spiritual detachment. For the survivor the problem is more difficult. He too must maintain detachment; he too must preserve an identity apart from the one imposed by his environment. But since for him death is the immediate determinant of behavior, he must find a realm of separateness not in mind only but also in action. The survivor must act on two levels, be "with and against," as Eugen Kogon says. And what this means in practice is that to stay alive survivors often worked for, or even in, camp administration. As a Soviet survivor said, "you can only survive on a function" (Ekart, 53). To one degree or another, many survivors were spokes in the wheel of mass murder, the ultimate instance being those members of the *Sonderkommandos* who ran the Nazi gas chambers—but who also burned down Treblinka and Sobibor, and blew up the crematorium at Auschwitz.

Under normal circumstances, assistance in crime is condemned, if only because (and this amounts to a definition of the civilized state) there is always a margin of choice, always another way to live. But in extremity there may be no other way to live. In the concentration camps, to choose life means to come to terms with, but also to resist, the forces of destruction. And although this imperative opens the door to every manner of hypocrisy and lie, and therefore becomes a permanent occasion for corruption, it cannot be avoided. The luxury of sacrifice—by which I mean the strategic choice of death to resolve irreconcilable moral conflicts —is meaningless in a world where any person's death only contributes to the success of evil.

Overtly the survivor defers to death, covertly he or she defies it. This duality of behavior, of concrete action on separate levels, is one of the principal characteristics of existence in extremity—or in any institution, slavery for example, which through threat and force attempts to reduce its members to nothing but functions in the system. The structure of behavior in "total institutions" has been analyzed by Erving Goffman in *Asylums,* and he arrives at the following distinction:

> When an individual co-operatively contributes required activity to an organization and under required conditions . . . he is transformed into a co-operator; he becomes the "normal," "programmed," or built-in member. He gives and gets in an appropriate spirit what has been systematically planned for, whether this entails much or little of himself.

. . . I shall speak in these circumstances of the individual having a *primary adjustment* to the organization. . . .

I have constructed this clumsy term in order to get to a second one, namely, *secondary adjustments,* defining these as any habitual arrangement by which a member of an organization employs unauthorized means, or obtains unauthorized ends, or both, thus getting around the organization's assumptions as to what he should do and get and hence what he should be. Secondary adjustments represent ways in which the individual stands apart from the role and the self that were taken for granted for him by the institution (188-89).

Goffman concludes by suggesting that "these [secondary adjustments] together comprise what can be called the *underlife* of the institution, being to a social establishment what an underworld is to a city" (199). In extremity this "underlife" becomes the literal basis of life.

During the ordeal of the Warsaw Ghetto, for example, and precisely in Goffman's sense, Chaim Kaplan made the following remark in his *Diary:*

In these days of our misfortune we live the life of Marranos. Everything is forbidden to us, and yet we do everything. Every Jewish occupation is under a ban, yet nevertheless we somehow support ourselves; true, we do it with grief, but we do survive (174).

Trade was illegal, procuring medicines was illegal, schooling the children was illegal. So were things like meetings, movement outside the ghetto, and traveling the streets after curfew. The punishment was death, and yet all these activities were necessary to life and had to be carried on covertly, at constant risk.

One of the most persistent forms of "secondary adjustment," in both the camps and the ghettos, was smuggling. In the Warsaw Ghetto this kind of "illegal" activity involved everyone; it proceeded daily on both individual and organized levels, and as death by starvation increased, it grew to heroic proportions. There were periodic crackdowns, when dozens of smugglers were shot, and other, looser times when bizarre methods of every sort were used:

> Specially constructed mobile ramps were set against the walls on both sides to smuggle over live cows and oxen. . . . From the window of a building . . . which overlooked the ghetto . . . a sheet metal pipe was lowered and milk poured across the racial boundary (Goldstein, 78).

Operations on this scale depended on collaboration with the oppressor—in other words, on "one simple and powerful mechanism, bribery, which reached to the police of all varieties and the gendarmes of all ranks" (Goldstein, 75). The complexity of such deals was amazing, as in this example from Ringelblum's *Notes:*

> A ladder is thrown over the Wall and smuggling goes on all night. But this night the smugglers quarrel among themselves, and one of them informs where it will do the most good. The police come at once and catch a whole crowd in the middle of operations. Machine guns begin shooting, one smuggler is shot dead on the spot, one or two others wounded. Then they search every apartment in the building, take away a great deal of goods,

and arrest forty smugglers. For 40,000 zlotys, they return the goods and set the smugglers free. That is the sum that the police claim to have lost because the smugglers used the Wall to bring goods in, rather than taking them through the watch at the Ghetto gate, where the police get a cut (264-65).

Organized smuggling brought profits, and no doubt that was a powerful incentive. But Ringelblum observed a devil-may-care attitude among smugglers, a kind of stark bravado which kept them going and gave their deeds a desperate glamor: "One of the smugglers told a friend that he would keep on smuggling, because if he didn't, he would starve to death. Rather die fast from a bullet than slow from hunger" (293). For the children, however, glamor faded to pathos, a pathos infinite and never to be answered, as in this example from Mary Berg's *Diary:*

Whole gangs of little children are organized, boys and girls from five to ten years of age. The smallest and most emaciated of them wrap burlap bags around their bony little bodies. Then they slink across to the "Aryan" side. . . . Often peasants give them potatoes for nothing. Their terrible appearance arouses pity. . . . On this side of the barbed wire their older partners wait for them. Very often they stay there for hours waiting until the Nazi guard is busy checking the passport of some foreign citizen or Polish Gentile visiting the ghetto. This gives them an opportunity to smuggle their foodstuffs. Sometimes the German sentry does not notice them, sometimes he does, but pretends that he does not. . . . But most of the German guards

fire in cold blood at the running children, and the
Jewish policemen must then pick up the bleeding
victims, fallen like wounded birds, and throw them
on passing rikshas (72-73).

Here we should also remember—especially when we
talk about people dying "like sheep"—that any kind of
armed uprising within the ghettos or the camps depended on smuggling; and that arms were a great deal
harder to obtain, and certainly harder to hide, than
food. When Bruno Bettelheim criticizes everyone in
Auschwitz who did not act as did the *Sonderkommando*
which blew up the crematorium and shot it out with the
SS (Nyiszli, "Foreword"), he does not allow for the
fact that the arms and explosives which made that particular revolt possible took *years* to accumulate. An
organization had to be forged and made trustworthy
amid constant depletion of members who were killed.
Contacts with partisan groups outside the camp had to
be made and, more difficult yet, maintained through
time against informers. Finally, arms had to be found,
paid for (which involved another network of smuggling), and successfully carried through an intricate system of surveillance. Only then was revolt possible. And
all this had to be done while, ostensibly, the prisoners
were cringing like dogs before their Nazi masters.

They cringed and hurried to perform their ugly jobs,
but they did not justify themselves by saying, "I *do* one
thing but *I think* another." The survivor is not a type
of the "beautiful soul," as Hegel called those who embrace pristine principles but dare not tarnish them
through action. Inward resistance is indispensable, but
for survivors something more is needed. Their lives and
humanness directly depend on active *works*. And since
on the "primary" level they are meshed in destruction,

they must find another, "secondary" level of action—
ways which will keep themselves and each other alive
in spirit as well as in body. Survivors often remark that
if a prisoner were to obey all camp rules he or she would
be dead in a month. As a woman who survived Auschwitz says, "According to even the Camp Commandant . . . the obedient *Häftlinge* could only survive for
three months at the very most. Those who lived longer
did so only by cheating the authorities" (Hart, 66). Or
as a survivor of Buchenwald says, they "gradually realized that obedience meant death. The only hope of survival lay in resistance" (Weinstock, 34).

Ghetto and camp regulations were designed to make life
impossible. Survival therefore depended on an "underworld" of activities, all of them illegal, all of them risky,
but all essential to life. There was a special word for
this, current in all the camps: to carry out any kind of
illegal action was "to organize." As one survivor says,
"I was later to know that 'organize' was *the* most important word in the Auschwitz language. It meant: to
steal, buy, exchange, get hold of" (Hart, 54). Another
survivor, also from Auschwitz, gives a fuller description:

> In the language of a political prisoner the word
> "organize" means to acquire a thing you need with-
> out wronging another prisoner. For instance: to
> take a shirt from a warehouse full of underwear
> left to rot and be gnawed by rats because a Ger-
> man Kapo would rather see it destroyed than give
> it to prisoners is to organize. But to take someone
> else's shirt which she washed and put on the grass
> to dry is not to organize—that is stealing. When

a prisoner gives other prisoners a few loaves of bread filched from the supply room—this is organization. But when the block supervisor takes loaves from the rations of other prisoners and hands them out to privileged prisoners, for some underhand additional services—that is theft. On the area of the camp there are many storerooms filled with all kinds of goods. From time to time their contents are sent to the interior of Germany. To manage to get at those shipments and distribute some articles of daily need over the camp uncaught, and thus make life easier for fellow prisoners means to know how to organize (Szmaglewska, 66-67).

Food had to be organized, because no one could subsist on camp rations. Things like shoes, blankets and warm clothing had to be organized, as did jobs. Spoons and bowls—without which one could not even get soup —had to be organized, because in many cases these essential items were not provided. And although on occasion the individual prisoner had a chance to grab something for himself, most of the time the items of daily need could only be acquired through collective action; hence the social significance of the word *organize,* used to cover all forms of illegal, life-sustaining activity. This was one of the primal facts about Auschwitz, or any of the camps, and it was something the new prisoner had to learn fast if he or she expected to live:

And all the time there was this awful fight for one's bare existence. The essential thing, of course, was not to lose the will to live, for this definitely meant death. I soon realized that alone one could not possibly survive. It was necessary therefore to form little families of two or three. In this way we looked after one another (Hart, 63).

The most important kind of organizing (apart from that of the political underground) was smuggling food, shoes and clothing out of warehouses into the rest of the camp. The Nazi extermination plant included gigantic systems of storage and transport, places where the belongings of millions of victims—money and foodstuffs, blankets, cooking utensils and all kinds of clothing— were gathered and packed for shipment back to the Reich. The largest of these was at Auschwitz. It was called "Canada," which in camp slang meant "an abundance of everything." There was so much sheer bulk to be processed that "the Germans became generous with manpower and put nearly twelve hundred men and two thousand women into the work" (Lengyel, 77). And although the least punishment a prisoner could expect for "stealing" was the customary and often fatal twenty-five lashes, each evening members of the Canada squads returned with vital loot:

> One had six tins of sardines, another, two pounds of figs. Shirts and fruit and soap, salami, sausages and ham appeared until the barracks began to look like a well-stocked grocery. . . . The block senior strolled in to collect his percentage. . . . The camp doctors, themselves prisoners, were there, too, looking for drugs, for medicines, for anything which might help them in their hopeless task (Vrba, 132).

The crucial moment was the search, and all kinds of tricks were devised to get through:

Every evening, before returning to camp, we were put through three spot-checks. These were carried out by dead-drunk Storm Troopers. . . . Anyone on whom was found the smallest trifle was beaten terribly. . . . Even so, everyone smuggled things back into camp. . . . Every day I put on a new pair of shoes at work, came back wearing them and gave them to comrades in the camp. . . . We smuggled gloves, blouses, underwear on our stomachs, under the coarse striped camp chemise. I hid pieces of bread, cake, bacon under my clothing as I held it during the searches (Birenbaum, 169-70).

Each Canada worker had his or her own special methods, on which the lives of others depended: "I usually wore at least three of everything. . . . I pinned towels along the inside back of the dresses. . . . I carried rings and even gold watches inside my mouth" (Hart, 95).

Such places as Canada were like infernal funnels through which the wealth of the victims was sucked in—tons of gold, millions of dollars in jewelry—supposedly to be sent to Berlin, but much going into SS pockets. Some of it, however, went for purposes far different from those prescribed:

We used the bank notes as toilet paper. We buried boxes full of gold and valuables in the ground. We handed much to the men, if and whenever possible, for it was generally believed that the men had contact with an underground movement and that any valuables might come in useful in obtaining ammunition for an uprising (Hart, 88).

Smuggling is only one example of "organizing." Prisoners working in factories performed daily acts of sabotage and theft. Those who worked in the notorious medical blocks stole medicines, jockeyed names, lied about symptoms, and in Buchenwald they used the typhus wards, which the SS would not go near, to hide men whose names had come up on the death lists. Others kept up contact with partisan groups and helped arrange escapes. Still others circulated news of the progress of the war—news on which camp morale depended. In Soviet camps there was mass theft of camp supplies, especially coal and construction materials, both essential to survival in an arctic climate. Camp facilities were used for "illegal" activities: "Buildings designed for the manufacture of heavy equipment also housed independent workshops for producing goods out of pilfered materials, waste, and remnants" (Gilboa, 197). And since, in the Soviet camps, the worker's daily food allotment, as well as the privileges of those in administration, depended on fulfillment of "work norms," everyone, from the common worker to the Camp Commandant, falsified work reports. Prisoners fulfilled their timber-cutting norm by stealing from yesterday's output. If a work brigade produced fourteen cars of coal in a day, the brigade leader put down fifteen in his report, in order to meet the norm and insure a decent food allotment for his men. In GULAG, cheating was universal.

The distinction between "primary" and "secondary" levels of behavior was central to the concentration-camp experience. Men and women conformed because otherwise they died. But they also resisted, and for the same reason: otherwise they died. Only by resisting could they sustain themselves and each other through despair and hardship. As a survivor of Auschwitz puts it:

Oppression as violent as that under which we lived automatically provoked resistance. Our entire existence in the camp was marked by it. When the employees of "Canada" detoured items destined for Germany to the benefit of their fellow internees, it was resistance. When labourers at the spinning mills dared to slacken their working pace, it was resistance. When at Christmas we organized a little "festival" under the noses of our masters, it was resistance. When, clandestinely, we passed letters from one camp to another, it was resistance. When we endeavoured, and sometimes with success, to reunite two members of the same family—for example, by substituting one internee for another in a gang of stretcher bearers—it was resistance (Lengyel, 154).

On the surface, cooperation with camp administration appeared total. But underneath, moral sanity reasserted itself, response to necessity was characterized by resistance, and the worst effects of extremity were thereby transcended. In a literal sense, these countless, concrete acts of subterfuge constituted the "underlife" of the death camps. By doing what had to be done (disobey) in the only way it could be done (collectively) survivors kept their social being, and therefore their essential humanity, intact.

The effectiveness of "organizing" depended on teamwork, and stable social units were thereby created in which relations were personal and friendly. These small groups sprang up everywhere, but in addition there was another, much broader network of interaction. This was the black market, an impersonal system of acquisition and barter which ran full tilt in all the concentration camps. Like any black market, this one took advantage of privation and thrived on scarcity. It was exceptional only in the scope and daring of its operations, and perhaps also for the improbable items —bottles of Clos Vougeot, caviar, packs of Lucky Strike—which appeared as if by magic. Goods were acquired in all sorts of ways, from "organizing" and manufacture to theft and deals with guards and camp officials. Elaborate methods of trading evolved, many of them dangerous and all of them open to betrayal. Yet here was a vigorous underworld of interchange. Prisoners met as buyers and sellers, sometimes in friendship, more often in suspicion and cunning, but nevertheless as participants in a steady stream of activity which, in the end and despite grave abuse, supported the general struggle for life. A survivor of Auschwitz describes it this way:

> Prices were determined by the scarcity of commodities, the inadequacy of rations, and, of course, by the risks in securing the article. . . . The barter was a natural result of local conditions. It was difficult not to take part in it. I paid eight days' ration of bread for a piece of cloth to make a nurse's blouse. I also had to pay three soups to have it sewn (Lengyel, 78-79).

This was the underside of the underside, a dimension of "secondary" action which exploited vital needs but at the same time helped to fulfill them. And it was important for another reason. By playing on SS greed, the black market contributed to the spread of corruption in high places; and this, in turn, weakened the discipline of the SS, not only among themselves, but more importantly in their control of camp affairs and therefore the lives of the prisoners. "Large-scale theft was possible," says a survivor of Auschwitz, "only because S.S. men and women, who were supposed to supervise the prisoners at their work in the stores, stole themselves, in competition and accord with the prisoners" (Lingens-Reiner, 48). Power declined as guards and officers came more and more to depend on their victims:

> For instance, the camp doctor, Dr. Rohde, before going on leave which he was spending with his wife, went to a Polish prisoner and asked the man to find him a nice present for her. What he got was a large pigskin dressing-case. When he returned from leave he told the prisoner that his wife had liked it very much and sent many thanks (Lingens-Reiner, 48).

The by-ways of trade and theft were often quite complicated, and sometimes even humorous:

> I remember the round trip of a pair of battle-dress trousers. An S.S. man stole them from a comrade and sold them for stolen sugar to a prisoner working in the kitchen. The prisoner gave them to his girl friend in the woman's camp from whom they were stolen by another prisoner, a prostitute. Another S.S. man "confiscated" them as "illicit property," and gave them to a second prostitute with whom he had an affair. She sold them for spirits to a wardress, who bartered them for margarine, after which they returned to the first prisoner working in the men's kitchen. . . . So it happened with small things and with far more important things. And perhaps it was not alto-

gether an evil, because even a black market is better than none at all (Lingens-Reiner, 46).

Relatively few prisoners had the energy and time for intrigue of that sort. Traffic in "illicit property" touched the rest of the camp population mainly on the level of small thefts, and these were so constant and widespread as to constitute a perpetual mode of exchange:

> The uniformed SS Doctor Koenig rushes among the standing women. . . . Bowls and spoons fly with a clash, bread, rations of margarine and sausage end in the ditch. . . . From behind the brick barracks gypsies cautiously creep out. . . . In one second the ditch is empty, and the property has changed hands (Szmaglewska, 71).

In the Soviet camps, stealing was nothing less than *the* way of life. As one survivor says:

> Stealing was prevalent . . . in every camp in Russia. For eight years I never heard any denial of this. It could not be called dishonesty: it was simply a fight for life at any price (Ekart, 204).

The point is not so much the prevalence of stealing as the fact that amid this scramble of trickery and theft a semblance of order emerged—conditions of interchange which were tolerated in much the same way as we, when we play games, agree to abide by the "rules." Through practices that could be justified only by extreme need, a system of barter became possible, a partial recovery of human community through inhuman means. The wonder is not that a black market thrived or that stealing was rampant, but that these activities did not thrive more, did not become absolute. There was in all the camps a significant drive toward decency, a persistent tendency to transcend the amorality of initial conditions and to establish modes of interchange which were life-supporting and a basis for relations truly social:

> Small cooperatives were formed. One member contributed his kettle, another some water, a third a slice of bread and another a pinch of salt. The biggest capitalist of all was Joachim . . . who had hidden away in his underwear a small packet of saccharine tablets. Breaking each tablet in half, and sometimes into quarters, he would give a piece to the cooperatives in exchange for a good share of the brew. But I did all right too. I had a little bar of concentrated pea soup, so everyone was willing to do business with me (Fittkau, 121).

This kind of "business" was universal and was governed by "one of the basic laws of prison-camp life":

> Any small possessions that others might use became a man's capital and he was entitled to make profit from them. A knife earned you a sliver of any food it was used to cut. A needle could be rented for anything the man who wanted to use it could pay (Fittkau, 84).

Pushed by necessity, prisoners became masters of invention; they acquired items useful for camp "business" by an endless proliferation of cunning and ingenious techniques:

> To begin with first things: you want a needle in prison, if you are to keep your clothes and socks

—don't forget you have no change of clothing—in any sort of repair. But you have no tools; everything has been taken away from you. What you do then is to smash the light bulb . . . and from the fragments select a sharp, pointed piece of glass. With that you can bore a hole through a fishbone and there is your needle (Knapp, 29).

Or consider the use of the latrine in a Soviet prison:

There were a few loose bricks in the wall, which were excellent for sharpening bits of metal. In this way we were able to make the tools necessary for our continued existence. . . . As knives and needles were needed by all, . . . the majority had to borrow them, and the service was repaid by some makhorka [tobacco], a piece of bread or some sugar (Ekart, 26).

And as in any system of manufacture and services, methods of distribution were also invented:

The next step was the division of the bread into the required number of portions, which was done by a man specially elected for that function. . . . The sugar was also divided out with the aid of scales made from matchboxes, wood and pieces of string. But as even with all these precautions there was no guarantee that the shares would be equal, lots were drawn in the following manner. The rations of bread and sugar were divided into batches for five people and then placed on the table. Then five people messing together would appoint a delegate, who was given a number for his group. One delegate would stand with his back to the table, and another would point at a group of rations and say,

"For whom?" The one with his back to the table might say, "Number twelve," which meant that the delegate from number twelve group would collect the particular lot of rations and divide it with his four messmates (Ekart, 28-29).

Next to food, the most prized commodity for trade, especially in the Soviet camps, was tobacco—not tobacco such as we know, but "the well-known Russian *makhorka* (a special plant-stem cut into small pieces), which tastes right only when it is wrapped up in Russian newspaper, as this does not burn while smoking, but only glows" (Nork, 32). Almost all prisoners came to use this stuff, not only because "it was an excellent remedy against hunger" (Nork, 32), but also because in extreme deprivation some slight pleasure is imperative, some physical stimulation indispensable—not to mention the psychic lift that such a drug can produce when the body is starving. To say that tobacco served a steady social function is not to exaggerate:

There was no such thing as matches or flint, but the prisoners had an ingenious system of their own for lighting the cigarettes. A fellow named Vasha was a past master at the technique. He was also jealous of his talent, because he exacted two puffs from every cigarette he lit. He'd take a piece of cotton, or stuffing from a pillow, or the lining of a quilted jacket, fluff it up and stretch it out very thin, then roll it up tight. Next he would put the cotton between two boards and rub them vigorously, faster and faster, sometimes for as long as fifteen minutes. . . . As soon as he smelled smoke, Vasha pulled out the rolled-up cotton, broke it at the point where it was smoldering, and very gently began to blow on it until it was completely aglow. Then, while he carefully shielded it in his hand, everyone who had a cigarette crowded eagerly around for a light. Vasha would take the first two puffs from every cigarette, drawing the smoke deep down into his lungs on each puff until it looked as if he were about to burst, hold the smoke as long as he could, then exhale it—into someone else's mouth (Ciszek, 91).

Strange practices, but organized with ritual correctness, with division of labor and reward. In the camps any kind of talent, any sort of item or possession, was put to enterprising use. Prisoners became expert scavengers, forever on the lookout for anything at all—"a piece of tinplate, a nail, a stick or a cigarette end" (Ekart, 32)—with which to transact "business." In *One Day in the Life of Ivan Denisovich,* Solzhenitsyn's hero risks severe punishment to smuggle a piece of broken saw-blade past the guards. He knows that sooner or later another prisoner will be "in the market" and ready to trade. On such modes of exchange survivors depended for a life that was primitive and barren, but not without dignity, and not completely savage. Always on the verge of social dissolution, men and women managed to achieve sustaining order through forms of interchange which life itself—in all things the mother of invention—demanded of them.

Between conditions in Soviet and in Nazi camps there were obvious differences; and some of the latter, furthermore, were "official" killing centers while others were "merely" labor camps. Yet I have not hesitated to call all these places "death camps." More than three million people died in Auschwitz, but if the incoming prisoner was not killed immediately, his or her chance for life was much better than that of the prisoner sent to one of the smaller camps where there was less food and more random killing. And what, really, is the difference if Buchenwald was not classified as an exter- mination camp and had no gas chamber, but had special rooms for mass shooting and a level of privation so severe that prisoners died in hundreds every day? Star- vation claimed victims by the thousands everywhere. Apart from that, Nazi victims were usually gassed or shot, whereas Soviet prisoners died mainly of exhaustion and sickness. There was likewise a difference in atmo- sphere: horror and dread were overwhelming in the Nazi camps, while in Soviet camps the predominant mood was a blend of rage and hopelessness. But again, these are secondary distinctions so far as survivors are concerned. For them any camp was a closed world in which one's chance of coming through was nearly zero.

To describe existence in the camps as a condition of life-in-death is neither to exaggerate nor to fall back on metaphor. To preserve life survivors had to use the means at their disposal; they had to manipulate facilities within the camp itself, and chief among these were functionary jobs which, if strategically used, became a principal weapon of defense. Occupying such a position made the prisoner less vulnerable to chance and "selec- tion"; it also meant better food and shelter; and finally it allowed a vital margin of influence in situations where camp policy was carried out by the prisoners them- selves. "You must get yourself a 'function,'" said one Soviet inmate to a newcomer, "it is your only chance" (Ekart, 61). And as Eugen Kogon observes, "there were few long-time concentration-camp inmates who did not in the course of time rise to more favourable, if not comfortable, working conditions. Those who failed in this endeavour simply perished" (85).

And how did one "rise"? By chance and intrigue; by being around after others had died off or, once the political underground gained control, by being chosen as a man or woman likely to be of use in resistance operations. If the incoming prisoner had a craft, his or her chances were immeasurably better than average, since all kinds of skilled workers, from electrician to glassblower to cabinetmaker, were in constant demand. The one thing needful was a job which kept the prisoner away from "general work assignment" where inmates were inevitably shot or beaten to death. One might therefore work as a tailor, be a room orderly or a file clerk, a mechanic or a shoemaker. Many new prisoners were advised by seasoned inmates to lie: to say they knew carpentry or chemistry when they knew nothing of the sort. Thereby they avoided the first mass extermination and had time to either find or learn a skill that would keep them alive. No job ensured survival, but anything helped. Some, like laundry detail, were valuable mainly to the prisoners who held them. Others, like working in Canada, benefited a wider circle of inmates. And others, as we shall see, were used by the "political" prisoners (members of underground resistance groups) to take a hand in their own fate, to gain a degree of control and thereby save thousands of lives.

The conditions of life-in-death forced a terrible paradox upon survivors. They stayed alive by helping to run the camps, and this fact has led to the belief that prisoners identified not with each other but with their oppressors. Survivors are often accused of imitating SS behavior. Bruno Bettelheim has argued that "old prisoners" developed "a personality structure willing and able to accept SS values and behavior as its own"

(169). But that needs clarification, for in order to act like an SS man the prisoner had to occupy a position of real power. A cook could lord it over other prisoners, a locksmith could not. Among *Kapos,* block-leaders and other high camp functionaries, there were indeed prisoners who accepted SS standards as their own—this man for instance:

His speciality was strangling prisoners with the heel of his boot, and he would stand erect in the pose of a Roman gladiator, enjoying the approval of the other Kapos, who would speak admiringly of a "good, clean job" (Donat, 179).

Almost certainly, however, that man had been a killer before he came to the camps. For prisoners like him the camps did not cause brutality so much as simply endorse it. Bettelheim's observations are based on camp conditions in the late 1930's, a time when positions of power were held exclusively by criminals—by men and women who, prior to imprisonment, had been murderers, prostitutes, thieves. The concentration camps had long been a dumping ground for criminals, both in Russia and in Germany, and in the Nazi camps this type was exploited by the SS as the most suitable channel for the delegation of power.

But this is not a case of imitation: such prisoners were like their masters from the start. The Nazis knew their own kind and naturally established an order reflecting SS values. That criminals had so much power was one of the most deadly conditions in the camp world; and only slowly, through years of intrigue, threat, bribery and assassination, were underground resistance groups able to replace the criminal *Kapos* with men of their own. This kind of maneuvering was most successful in Buchenwald, least effective in the Soviet camps. One of the cardinal facts about the camps was that everywhere a battle raged between the "greens" and the "reds"—between those imprisoned for real crimes and those imprisoned for opposition to the regime.

The assumption that survivors imitated SS behavior is misleading because it generalizes a limited phenomenon, but also because it overlooks the duality of behavior in extremity. Eugen Kogon, a member of the Buchenwald underground, points out that "the concentration-camp prisoner knew a whole system of mimicry toward the SS," an "ever-present camouflage" which concealed true feelings and intentions (283). *Strategic* imitation of the SS was enormously important because thereby political prisoners held positions of power which would otherwise have gone to the criminals. In the following instance, a new prisoner, a baker, is attacked by a passing SS guard:

> With purely animal rage, he pulled off the baker's upper garments and tore them to shreds, and then whipped his bare back until the blood oozed. . . . Then the overseer, a Czech-German "political," noticed what was going on. He immediately rushed over and began shouting, "You goddamned Jewish dog! You'll work for the rest of the day without clothes! I'm sick of the trouble you lousy Jews give me!" He made a threatening gesture, and then roared, "Come with me!"
>
> The SS guard left, confident that the baker was in good hands. Then the overseer took the baker into a tool-shed where it was warm, dressed him, washed his wounds, and gave him permission to stay in the shed until it was time to quit work (Weinstock, 156-57).

Or take Franz, the *Kapo* of the SS storeroom in Auschwitz. Every day crates of food were "accidentally" dropped and reported as "shipment damage." The contents were then "organized"—for Franz, for his men and others in need. In the "open," however, there was another Franz:

> As we walked . . . past other kapos and SS men he began roaring at us. . . . As he shouted, he swung at us with his club. To the passing SS men he looked and sounded a splendid kapo, heartless, brutal, efficient; yet never once did he hit us (Vrba, 90).

Imitation of SS behavior was a regular feature of life in the camps, and large numbers of prisoners benefited because positions of power were secretly used in ways which assisted the general struggle for life. Even small jobs—working as a locksmith for instance—dovetailed into the larger fabric of resistance:

> We had access to more and better food, and were able to keep ourselves clean; we had sufficient clothing and footwear. In due time we were able to assist other prisoners. . . . We locksmiths had special passes . . . from the camp authorities. With these we were able to go outside the camp and also to visit the other camps at Birkenau. . . . Often enough we merely pretended to work. Many were the good door handles and locks that we unscrewed and screwed up again at the approach of an SS man. If we were to work effectively as contacts between the various resistance groups it was essential that we should be able to hang about in this way, especially when we needed information from

other camps or when something unusual was going on (Kraus and Kulka, 2).

The most important jobs were in administration offices. Here is Kogon's description of the "Orderly Room" in Buchenwald:

Its entire personnel was made up of prisoners. It took care of all internal camp administration— files, assignment of barracks, preparation for roll call, ration distribution, etc. It was an institution of great importance to a camp, and for the most part its achievements were constructive. It is no exaggeration to say that in the course of the years the Orderly Room preserved the health and lives of literally thousands of inmates, maneuvering many into positions where they could do effective work on behalf of their fellows (61).

Another "citadel of prisoner power" was the "Labor Records Office," which was a hotbed of vengeance and intrigue, but which also functioned to save the lives of hundreds of prisoners, "either . . . secretly scratched from death shipments, or . . . smuggled into outside labor details when their life was in danger in camp" (Kogon, 62). The "Camp Police" was another branch of administration used to the inmates' advantage. They carried out all orders to the letter, but in subtly subversive ways, and whenever possible with a less than lethal rigor: "thousands of prisoners would have fared infinitely worse . . . had not this prisoner cadre provided an impeccable camouflage of discipline toward the SS" (Kogon, 65).

Of all camp institutions, the one most consistently used to save lives was the camp "hospital." To appreciate the work of prisoners in the medical blocks, it must be understood that the official function of camp hospitals was not at all to save lives. Simply to go in was dangerous, as we have seen, and yet just here the paradox of life-in-death is most clear:

In every concentration camp where the political prisoners attained any degree of ascendancy, they turned the prisoner hospital, scene of fearful SS horrors that it was, into a rescue station for countless prisoners. Not only were patients actually cured wherever possible; healthy prisoners, in danger of being killed or shipped to a death camp, were smuggled on the sick list to put them beyond the clutches of the SS. In special cases, where there was no other way out, men in danger were nominally permitted to "die," living on under the names of prisoners who had actually died (Kogon, 141).

Exchanging the living for the dead was a common practice in Nazi camps. Another tactic was called "submerging": prisoners singled out for extermination would be hidden, sometimes for months, in the tuberculosis and typhus wards, which were places of relative safety because the SS were afraid to enter them. Still another tactic was to pad the order-list for medicines: after it had been signed by an SS officer, but before it left for Berlin, "the list wandered through the typewriter, to emerge with some changes, allowances having previously been made for spaces" (Poller, 243). And all these practices were carried through, day in and day out, by men and women who knew they would be shot if caught.

Arrangements as complex as those just described took

a high degree of coordination and were extensive only in camps where a political underground had had time to form. Most "maneuvers" in the medical blocks were simpler. Staff members allowed prisoners extra time to recover from exhaustion or sickness, or deliberately falsified diagnoses for cases which otherwise would automatically have been sent to the gas chamber. When sickness was prolonged, or when an individual prisoner was in special danger, he or she was moved from name to name, ward to ward:

> One morning . . . the *officerine* beat me, . . . shouting that she was going to send me . . . to my death. After she had left, the *blovoka* hurried over and took me into another ward. She put me in a bunk with the light behind me and pinned a new chart at its foot. In this way I was able to pass for another patient (Maurel, 51).

Tactics like these were successful because with thousands of prisoners coming and going, all looking alike, the authorities could not possibly keep track of everything and everyone. In some cases prisoners were actually able to move from camp to camp, a situation the political underground regularly exploited to start or shore up resistance movements elsewhere: "They assigned a lot of dead people to the transports. They never knew who was dead, who was alive. We picked out a few dead ones and changed their numbers for our own. Then we reported to the proper transport" (Weinstock, 169). Prisoners took full advantage of loopholes, death was manipulated in favor of life, and the minimal latitude thus obtained was increased by another small circumstance: a large number of SS men were drunk much of the time. That was another crack through which life seeped.

In extremity life depends on solidarity. Nothing can be done or kept going without organizing, and inevitably, when the social basis of existence becomes self-conscious and disciplined, it becomes "political"—political in the elementary human sense, as in the following description by two survivors of Auschwitz:

> Unlimited egoism and a consuming desire to save their own lives at the expense of their fellows were common phenomena among prisoners who were politically backward, for such people were quite incapable of realizing that in this way they merely strengthened the hand of the SS against the prisoners. . . . Our experience of other concentration camps [prior to Auschwitz] had taught us the vital need to live collectively. Political consciousness and contact with others in the struggle against Nazism were necessary conditions of success; it was this that gave people a sense of purpose in life behind barbed wire and enabled them to hold out (Kraus and Kulka, 27, 1).

Prisoners were "politically backward" if they did not see that collective action is more effective than individual effort, or if they did not understand that solidarity becomes power in proportion to the degree of disciplined order. Many never understood, and theirs was "the tragedy of all people who live under the illusion that isolation is individualism":

The great "individualists" of our free days, the
unorganized and backward workers, the cynics,
not to mention business men who knew nothing of
organized action, . . . all disintegrated morally.
They became witless tools for the Nazis. They
groveled for favours although their groveling degraded them still further. And they did not live
long in Buchenwald (Weinstock, 125, 95).

Kogon observes that "the lone wolves here were always
especially exposed to danger" (280), and Bettelheim
has noted that "non-political middle class prisoners"
were among the first who "disintegrated as autonomous
persons" (120-21). Another survivor sums it up this
way: "survival . . . could only be a social achievement,
not an individual accident" (Weinstock, 74).

Human relations in the camps took as many forms as
they generally take. The most narrow but intense social
unit was the family; beyond that were old friends, and
beyond that a sense of collective identity among those
from the same town or area—bonds reinforced by the
earlier ordeal of deportation which all had suffered
together. Another strong basis for solidarity was na-
tionality. There are endless tales of the toughness of
national groups sticking together, and all survivors recall occasions when they received help from, or offered
help to, a stranger who was a fellow countryman. The
trouble with national allegiance, when it became a unit
of resistance, was that such groups vied among themselves for control of life-resources. Conflict on the level
of national groups only abated when the political underground, cutting across national barriers, became
strong enough to take command of resistance activities
throughout the camp.

In discussing the achievements of the political prisoners, what counts is not the different factions or differences in principle, but that as members of the underground they worked together, and that as time went on they achieved greater and greater power as an organized resistance movement. This was true mainly in the Nazi camps, however. In Soviet camps there was much "illegal" activity, and over time the rise of organized resistance did much to improve camp conditions and check at least the worst of abuses by criminal inmates. At the time of Stalin's death, furthermore, open revolt spread throughout GULAG—"strikes" in which whole camp populations refused to work or cooperate —especially in Vorkuta and the camps of Northern Kazakhstan. By contributing to the decay of official power, resistance of this sort saved many, perhaps millions, of lives; yet it cannot be compared to the kind of firmly established underground which operated in places like Dachau and Auschwitz or especially in Buchenwald where, by the end of the war, the political prisoners ran internal camp affairs completely. To speak of a resistance movement in the concentration camps is therefore to speak of a tendency, *a kind of logic or potential inherent in the social foundation of survival struggle*. In different camps this tendency was realized to different degrees. But where it did operate effectively it became the basis of life and was responsible for the survival of thousands of prisoners, including many who knew nothing of its existence. The situation in Ravensbrück was typical:

> The political prisoners displayed great daring and courage. For instance, the list of those who were condemned to the gas chamber occasionally was destroyed. Many prisoners don't know to this day

that they were sentenced to death and can thank their political leaders for saving their lives. These political prisoners also risked their own lives and undertook daily to make falsifications on the lists of the food allowances. They canceled out names in the work lists if their comrades happened to be ill. The name of an ill person would be exchanged for the name of a healthy person. When the prisoners were moved to other camps or to the execution places, there political prisoners hid many of them—some were even hidden among the corpses, which were lying in a cellar waiting to be cremated (Gluck, 66).

Unfortunately, political organization did not come into being all at once; nor was it coterminous with the beginnings of the camp system. In Ravensbrück effective resistance did not develop until late in the war. Here, as in all cases, time was the crucial factor. Years were required to create a reliable underground, years of bitter struggle and many deaths. Leaders were usually "political" in the strict sense, men and women imprisoned as early as 1933 for their opposition to the regime. As the war went on, large numbers of partisan fighters and POW's were swept into the camps. Prisoners like these had formed an attitude of resistance *before* imprisonment, and therefore came through the period of initial collapse faster and with less damage. They had no illusions about their predicament, and once they had agreed among themselves that survival was only possible through discipline, they set about their task with a rigor as ruthless as the enemy they opposed. They began by fighting it out with the criminals. At Auschwitz they did it this way:

The first tasks assumed by this group were to organize help for their weaker comrades and to exact better treatment from the Kapos. The means adopted for curbing the Kapos soon resulted in improved conditions. . . . The organization would select . . . a particularly vicious Kapo, . . . fall upon him at night, throw his corpse into the camp cesspool and leave him to be found in the morning (Kraus and Kulka, 21).

The next step was to expand their own ranks by finding men and women already aware of the need for resistance. This was accomplished by screening new arrivals, which in practice became a kind of "favoritism" toward certain prisoners. Thus a survivor of Buchenwald describes his first days:

When the boots were issued, I was about to be given a down-at-the-heels pair, when I was asked if I was a political; upon my replying that I was, a better pair of boots was substituted. Only we politicals, too, were asked if we had brought pullovers or woolen jackets with us, and those who had not were given these garments. All other categories of prisoners went without them (Poller, 35).

In extremity, items like boots and jackets are weapons. They keep the prisoner in better physical and mental shape, and thereby increase his capacity as a fighter. This was not, in other words, a question of favoritism at all, although it was resented as such by prisoners not aware of resistance efforts. The underground was fighting a war as real as any battle on the Western Front; and it was imperative to locate and preserve men and women already prepared to fight. For this reason "it was an unwritten, cast-iron law in the camp that special prisoners were to be protected" (Poller, 95). A prisoner was "special" precisely to the degree that he or she participated in resistance activities. Experienced members had to survive if the underground was to remain organized and effective. In the end everyone in camp would benefit.

Resistance efforts depended "on two essential prerequisites: power inside the camp, and a well-organized intelligence service" (Kogon, 230). Life depended on getting and spreading vital information, and systems of surveillance and communication sprang up in all the camps. Here is an example from Auschwitz:

> We needed to disseminate war news that would help to bolster the morale of the internees. After solving technical problems of enormous difficulty, our friend, L., thanks to the cooperation of the "Canada," succeeded in constructing a little radio set. The radio was buried. Sometimes late at night a few trusted ones hurried out to listen to an Allied newscast. This news was then broadcast by word of mouth as fast as possible (Lengyel, 155).

Monitoring the progress of the war was also a way to measure the morale of the SS, thus providing a kind of information increasingly valuable as the war neared its end. In order to pass news and messages—information personal as well as political—a system of covert communications spread between different sections of the camps. Locksmiths, electricians and other skilled workers provided this essential service:

The visitor asks for the chief, talks with him about some repairs to electric installations, examines the sockets, moves about here and there looking for a stool, for a ladder. You have to be thoroughly familiar with the camp and its affairs to understand that "repairs" serve mostly as a pretext to enter the women's camp and transact some sort of intimate business. The errand may be a personal one of the "repairman," or it may be for someone else. . . . An uninitiated observer will never notice the imperceptible gesture, lasting perhaps a fraction of a second, which is necessary to perform the mission on which this young man came. He may have brought a woman a letter. . . . He may have called for a letter. . . . He may have brought medicine acquired at the risk of his own life for some seriously sick person (Szmaglewska, 98-99).

The most important positions in the underground intelligence system were filled by prisoners working directly for the SS as messengers, file clerks, typists and the like:

There they were able to observe everything that happened in the ranks of the SS and the prisoners, to obtain information on every personnel shift and policy trend, to overhear every conversation. Everything that seemed of the slightest significance was under constant scrutiny. . . . A prisoner orderly might be unobtrusively sweeping out an office or a hall, apparently minding only his own business, the SS men never dreaming that his attention was focused on anything but the broom in his hand. It is no exaggeration to say that nothing of any importance happened in a concentration camp, including even secret information, that did not come to the attention of the prisoners either immediately or else in a very short time. All reports converged on the underground leaders and the circles around them (Kogon, 230).

Prisoners learned ahead of time about death lists, transports and SS policy shifts, and were thus able to avert or manipulate or at least lessen the destructive impact. Information of this kind was decisive in the last days of the camps, when the intentions of the SS were carefully monitored to forestall mass catastrophe. In Buchenwald the underground made contact with the Allies, resulting in a bombing raid which severely damaged SS sectors of the camp. It was also during this raid (August 24, 1944) that the underground began to arm itself: "Advantage was taken of the general confusion that reigned, and as many rifles, pistols, carbines and hand grenades as possible were removed from the SS division replacement depot. The weapons were carefully concealed" (Kogon, 248). Thus the foundation was laid for an eventual uprising, which culminated in the take-over of Buchenwald. The planned extermination of the camp, scheduled by the SS, never took place.

There could be only one uprising, of course, and it could happen only late in the war, when the SS was no longer certain of reinforcements from outside the camp. In general, therefore, resistance tactics, while steadily gaining strength for the final fight, were restricted to more humble efforts. Apart from the business of saving particular lives, one of the principal activities of the underground was sabotage, although here too only small deeds could be attempted, since any large-scale damage attributéd to the prisoners would have evoked mass reprisal:

> Generally speaking, sabotage had to assume forms that were hard to recognize. The primary possibility was manpower utilization. Naturally the prisoners preferred to assign skilled workers only to plants that were not directly concerned with arms production. The latter were sent mainly unskilled help. Reliable anti-Fascist experts, however, were wormed into positions where they could practice systematic sabotage. . . . As a result it was possible to conduct a comprehensive program of sabotage by means of faulty planning and building, delays in procuring machinery, tools and materials, fostering internal jurisdictional disputes, applying official regulations and test methods to the letter. . . . Such sabotage was by no means confined to the armament plants. It pervaded the whole structure of the concentration camps (Kogon, 243-44).

Another systematic effort on the part of the underground was to keep accurate records of everything, to provide safe hiding places for them, and to arrange escapes so that the rest of the world could know "what deportation really meant." Finally, in almost all the camps, the underground went out of its way to save children. In Buchenwald a Hungarian transport arrived containing four hundred and ten boys. Resistance leaders bargained with the SS and convinced them that if these young prisoners were allowed to live they would make excellent workers. At the same time, members of the underground were assigned to each boy individually, to provide food, clothing, and above all a sense of care: "On the day of liberation every child stood in the yard, alive and healthy. . . . This was Buchenwald's greatest miracle" (Weinstock, 193).

It was all miraculous, or no, it was not. God kept away from the concentration camps, and what was done, miraculous as it might seem, was done by human mind and will—by men and women doing what they could to make life possible. And their victories were never large: "In actual fact, their powers and opportunities were very limited. . . . They could only intervene in a few exceptional cases, and then only at the risk of their own lives" (Poller, 97). The enemy was infinitely more powerful, and the fight to survive was thus a kind of guerrilla warfare—small battles aimed at strengthening centers of defense. Members of the underground, furthermore, were not motivated by sentiment or faith in high causes. They were fighting for life on the principle that only through tight discipline and ruthless tactics was survival, and therefore help, possible. Resistance activities were governed by a "cold, unemotional, devastatingly logical approach to every problem" (Vrba, 193). And what this demanded of individual prisoners was the capacity to face moments of "hard choice." Life was saved by using death strategically, and this involved a moral dilemma which members of the underground simply had to accept and live with, no matter how difficult and cruel, no matter how hurtful to innocence.

In many of the Nazi camps, women who gave birth were automatically sent with their children to the ovens. To save at least *some* of these lives required the following decision by members of the hospital staff in Auschwitz: "One day we decided we had been weak long enough. We must at least save the mothers. To

carry out our plan, we would have to make the infants
pass for stillborn" (Lengyel, 99). The pain of such decisions was the price which members of the resistance
had to pay, just to salvage something rather than nothing in a world where, without this kind of hard choice,
all would have died:

And so, the Germans succeeded in making murderers of even us. To this day the picture of those
murdered babies haunts me. . . . The only meager
consolation is that by these murders we saved the
mothers. Without our intervention they would have
endured worse sufferings, for they would have been
thrown into the crematory ovens while still alive
(Lengyel, 100).

Death was thereby cheated, made less than absolute,
which is as much as survivors can hope for. They never
win, in a conventional sense, but only lose less than
all. And even to accomplish victories so small, so apparently insignificant against defeats so appalling, they
must make choices painful often past bearing. Many
could not bear it. They chose to die, rather than survive
on such terms. The hardness of the survivor's choice,
in other words, requires a toughness equal in its way to
the forces he or she resists; life goes on by using the
methods of the enemy.

Thus when lists were made up of prisoners to be
gassed or sent on especially dangerous work details, as
many places as possible were filled with criminals, informers or men lost in any case. The underground was
forced to make its own "selection" in strategic mimicry
of the Nazi procedure, and as one survivor says, "it was
the cruelest task that any Underground has ever faced.
. . . The Nazi system was so thorough that anti-Nazis,

too, had to use death as a tool" (Weinstock, 118). Here is another example: a young man breaks down when told of the death of his family. He decides that in the morning he will commit suicide by attacking an SS officer. Because of the Nazi practice of mass reprisal, his act will cost the lives of all four hundred men in his barracks (remember that the population of Lidice was wiped out because Heydrich, one of the SS high command, was assassinated by a man from that village). All night, therefore, the crazed man's comrades try to talk him back to sanity, but his grief is stronger than their appeals. So two members of the underground must decide:

> "Do you think he'd do it?"
> "I don't know. Maybe not. Maybe he'll calm down."

Maybe. Before roll-call next morning the camp hospital sent for the man, who was not seen again (Weinstock, 150). On the same principle, an informer who "did not shrink from denouncing anyone with whom he had ever had the most trivial dispute" got sick and was "unwise enough to report to the hospital" (Kogon, 229). He too disappeared.

Life was preserved because men and women did not hesitate when moments of hard choice arose. If, as happened at Auschwitz, some members of the resistance got caught, the rest of the organization had to be protected:

> If those men cracked under torture, it would mean more than their deaths, more than fierce reprisals against the rest of us. It would mean that the underground movement . . . would be liquidated. . . .

The leaders of the underground were fully aware of the danger and took swift evasive action. They smuggled poison into Block Eleven and within a few hours the men in Block Eleven were dead. Rather than risk revealing the names of their comrades, they had committed suicide (Vrba, 168-69)

As in any war, those who fight cannot afford sentiment. If one's comrade falls, that is that. The battle goes on, as did the smuggling of explosives in Auschwitz:

A young boy who only a day before had accepted a package from me swung on the gallows. One of my comrades, numb with fright, whispered to me, "Tell me, isn't that the same boy who was in the infirmary yesterday?"

"No," I replied. "I have never seen him before."

That was the rule. Whoever fell was forgotten (Lengyel, 156).

Compassion was seldom possible, self-pity never. Emotion not only blurred judgment and undermined decisiveness, it jeopardized the life of everyone in the underground. To oppose their fate in the death camps, survivors had to choose life at the cost of moral injury; they had to sustain spiritual damage and still keep going without losing sight of the difference between strategic compromise and demoralization. Hard choices had to be made and not everyone was equal to the task, no one less than the kind of person whose goodness was most evident, most admired, but least available for action:

It was the pure in heart who suffered the least damage . . . and . . . their lives shed radiance and beneficence on the rest of us. But on no account could they be placed in situations where they had to take part in making decisions vital to the very existence of the camp. . . . And the more tender one's conscience, the more difficult it was to make such decisions. Since they had to be made, and made swiftly, it was perhaps better that they should have fallen to the more robust spirits, lest all of us became martyrs instead of surviving witnesses (Kogon, 278).

The behavior of the political underground was always strategic. In each case the gain was weighed against the loss in a coldly logical manner: this much life cost that much death. For the majority of survivors, however, behavior was not based on reason and calculation. Most survivors simply found themselves helping each other, as if by instinct, as if in answer to a need. Their experience suggests, in fact, that when conditions become extreme a *need to help* arises; and there is no more terrible, nor more beautiful, instance than the way people helped each other during the days and weeks of the death marches. As the Eastern Front collapsed, camp after camp was evacuated: prisoners were driven into the winter dawn in endless columns, guarded by SS men hysterical with fear and viciousness. Whole camp populations were forced to walk across the frozen wastes of Poland into Germany, sometimes for weeks without food or even shoes. Those who fell behind or stopped for any purpose were shot, and at night many froze to death in their sleep. This last extremity pushed survivors to the limit of endurance, and here if anywhere self-interest made sense, each prisoner determined not to be dragged down now, so close to the end. But just here the testimony of survivors is full of examples of help—men and women giving a vital part of themselves, literally their last reserves, to keep each other going:

> My hand was frozen and the wound on it was endless torture. By now I was completely bent and dragged myself along with my two hands between my thighs. . . . A wearisome drowsiness possessed me; my knees gave way and I collapsed in the snow. . . . Someone was tugging at me and calling my name. "Let me sleep," I murmured. But the woman tugged harder, and through half-closed eyes I recognized Klari. "Please let me sleep, Klari," I begged. But she grabbed my arm and forced me to my feet (Weiss, 212).

That small event occurred innumerable times, and always at the risk of being singled out. Another kind of help, very simple but crucial, was keeping each other awake at night. With bodies so depleted and no place to sleep but in the snow, "sleep means death." And thus they joined in night-long vigilance:

> "Ilse!" I shook her.
> "Leave me alone!" she protested.
> "Ilse!" I shouted. "Wake up. You are not going to sleep!"
> She was awake now. I rubbed her face, her stiff hands. I called to Suse and Liesel. They responded. We passed the word around not to sleep. . . . We did everything we could think of to keep each other awake and encouraged (Klein, 188).

Staying awake was hard, but it was harder still to give physical support to someone who could no longer walk. A girl faints and falls, someone pulls her up. She regains consciousness and recognizes a member of the kitchen squad from Auschwitz: "She drew me to her still more strongly, and almost staggered under my weight. She herself was slender and quite frail" (Birenbaum, 219). Help reached its limit when survivors began to drag and carry their fallen friends:

> After an hour of indescribable distress, Benzi pleaded with us to drop him and leave him to his fate. We knew only too well that the line of S.S. marching at the rear would riddle his body with bullets once he was helpless. So near the end of our travails, how could we desert Benzi? We drew upon our reserves of strength and dragged him along for the remainder of that never-to-be-forgotten evening (Unsdorfer, 185).

Where such strength comes from, this last expense of energy among men and women themselves nearly dead, is the central mystery of life's resilience. Partly, prisoners on the death march knew the war was almost over and that *one* more effort was possible. Beyond that—and not forgetting that help regularly came from strangers—the need to help was rooted in bonds of friendship and loyalty forged earlier, during the months and years in camp, where by coming to owe each other their lives, survivors now felt the need to stick together no matter what. Having come this far, to repay what one owed seemed not too much, not beyond what those bound life to life are willing to attempt. And to speak of *owing life* is not, in extremity, mere metaphor. Smallest favors saved lives time and again.

Prisoners survived through concrete acts of mutual aid, and over time these many small deeds, like fibers in the shuttle of a clumsy loom, grew into a general fabric of debt and care. At roll-call, for instance, or *Appel,* as it was called in the Nazi camps, prisoners had to form up hours before dawn and stand at attention in thin rags through rain and snow. This occurred again in the evening, and took at least two hours, sometimes three and four, and every survivor remembers roll-calls which lasted all night. Prisoners had to stand there the whole time, caps off, caps on, as SS officers strolled past the ranks. Any irregularity was punished savagely, and irregularities were numerous. Prisoners fainted, collapsed from exhaustion and sickness, simply fell dead on the spot. "Those winter *Appels,*" says a survivor of Buchenwald, "were actually a form of extermination. . . . In addition to those who regularly fell dead during *Appel,* there were every day a number who contracted pneumonia and subsequently died" (Weinstock, 108).

To fall and be noticed by an SS man was to be beaten or shot, and the universal practice among prisoners was to use their own bodies to prop up inmates no longer able to stand. Almost all reports by survivors include moments at roll-call when an individual either gave, or was given, this kind of support: "I was so weakened that during roll call I could scarcely stay on my feet. But the others pressed close on either side and supported me with the weight of their bodies" (Szalet, 69). Or again:

Turning my face slightly over to the right, I saw the unconscious body of Federweiss propped up straight, squeezed tightly between the bodies of the two men in front and behind him. The man in the rear held him up by his trousers, while the one in

front pushed his back on Federweiss's chest to prevent him from dropping. They kept these positions
for quite a while—indeed until the S.S. man and
the *Blockaeltester* . . . were at a safe distance
(Unsdorfer, 104-5).

Help was forbidden, of course, but there was some
safety in numbers, for among so many thousands of
prisoners packed together, the SS could view any particular rank only briefly. But despite danger, the need
to help persisted, often in elaborate ways. It regularly
happened that sick prisoners were carried to roll-call
by comrades, who then took turns supporting them.
Sometimes this went on for days, and care for the sick
did not end with roll-call. Many men and women were
nursed back to health by friends who "organized" extra
food; who shuffled the sick man back and forth from
barracks to barracks; who propped him up at roll-call,
and kept him out of sight during "selections" and while
he was delirious. In one case a prisoner with typhus was
smuggled every day into the "Canada" work detail and
hidden in the great piles of clothing where he could
rest. This particular rescue involved getting the sick
man through a gate guarded by a *Kapo* whose job was
to spot sick and feeble prisoners and club them to death.
Each day, therefore, two prisoners supported the sick
man almost to the gate, and then left him to march
through on his own. Once past the guard they propped
him up again.

Prisoners in the concentration camps helped each
other. That in itself is the significant fact. Sometimes it
was help individually given, as in the case of a girl in
Birkenau who, "at the risk of being severely beaten if
her absence in the potato-peeling room was discovered,
every evening . . . brought coffee to the sick. The last

time she brought it was on the eve of her own death"
(Szmaglewska, 43). Sometimes it took the form of one
group helping another, as when a work squad had to
carry sacks of cement from the storeroom to a building
site:

> I was equal to the job, but working with us were
> weaker men who grew exhausted after a few trips.
> The younger of us, myself included, pitched in to
> help them. We had agreed among our group that
> we would help one another to whatever extent was
> possible, rather than surrender to the dog-eat-dog
> philosophy which poisoned the minds of some pris-
> oners (Weinstock, 154).

And sometimes help came collectively, unplanned and
uncalled for, where and when it was needed:

> For example, five women are pushing a conveyor
> car loaded to the brim with gravel. . . . the car
> jumps the track. . . . then it gets stuck in the sand.
> The women stop, completely helpless. Fortunately
> the chief is not around. All efforts to replace the
> car on the tracks are fruitless; the heavy-laden car
> will not budge and the chief may appear at any mo-
> ment. A clandestine congregating begins. Stealth-
> ily, bent fingers sneak toward the derailed car
> from all directions: the women who work on the
> mound of sand, those who level the gravel, a group
> just returned from delivering a track. A common
> exertion of arms and backs raises the car, the
> spades dig into the sand under the wheels and
> heave—and the loaded car moves, shivers. Fear
> gives strength to the workers. With more pushing,
> one wheel is on the track. A Kapo comes rushing

from afar, she has noticed people missing at various points of work. But before she can get there, one more tug, one more push—and the gravel-laden conveyor car proceeds smoothly along the tracks (Szmaglewska, 20-21).

The survivor's experience is evidence that the need *to* help is as basic as the need *for* help, a fact which points to the radically social nature of life in extremity and explains an unexpected but very widespread activity among survivors. In the concentration camps a major form of behavior was gift-giving. Inmates were continually giving and sharing little items with each other, and small acts like these were enormously valuable both as morale boosters and often as real aids in the struggle for life. Sometimes the gift was given outright, with no apparent relation between donor and receiver:

One evening we were served a soup made with semolina. I drank this with all the more relish since I often had to forgo the daily cabbage soup because of my bowels. Just then I noticed a woman, one of the prostitutes, who always kept very much to themselves, approaching my bunk, holding her bowl out to me with both hands.

"Micheline, I think this is a soup you can eat; here, take mine too."

She emptied her bowl into mine and went without food that day (Maurel, 21).

More often gifts came from friends or others in close association:

It was astonishing to see how anxious these hungry men were to share what they had. . . . There was half an orange on all the beds in the room. One of our friends had received a parcel. He had not even been able to wait for our return (Bernard, 90).

On her birthday, a member of the Auschwitz underground received a green apple and "a used toothbrush from which the bristles had been worn off on one end" (Lengyel, 139). Or finally there was just the delight of being *able* to give something, it did not matter what, as long as it was rare and distinctly a gift:

Ilse, who worked on the day shift, came back at noon. . . . She turned away from me so that I could not see what she was doing, and dug into her pocket. "I have brought you a present!" she announced triumphantly. There, on a fresh leaf, was one red, slightly mashed raspberry! (Klein, 175).

Prisoners acquired gift-items by chance and by organizing. In certain camps they received food parcels sent in from outside, and in all the camps things were to be got through the system of barter and exchange. In the following instance a prisoner in Auschwitz was able to get a loaf of bread from an SS man (many were deep in trade with prisoners) in return for a pack of cigarettes:

I was a rich man that night: the proud owner of a whole loaf of bread—not black camp bread, but bread prepared and baked for the elite of the German army. I was glad to share it with my friends on the night shift, but particularly to offer a fair share to Benzi, my friend, who had so often given me part of his bread and soup when my hunger

was unappeased by my own meager ration (Unsdorfer, 159-60).

As the foregoing example suggests, the gift was
usually food, and gift-giving thus became a mode of
distribution, a way of sharing vital wealth, based on the
elementary social act of reciprocity or mutual exchange.
Most often prisoners shared with those who shared with
them, and this practice was so firmly established that
one prisoner had a kind of right to share another's re-
sources—if, that is, he or she could contribute something of equal value in return. In a Soviet camp an
inmate shared a chunk of horse meat in the following
approved manner:

> I put the meat . . . on the small stove in our room.
> All my neighbors were highly interested. One of
> them, whom I knew only slightly, offered me a bit
> of salt, which I added to the water. When the meat
> was ready I invited him to share it with me. He
> contributed bread to the common repast (Gliks-
> man, 310).

Because they had nothing to exchange, or did not wish
to in this case, the other prisoners did not expect to
join in the meal. In the camp situation, furthermore,
salt was rare and valuable, and by offering it the donor
knew he was placing himself in a position to share the
other's food. But of course, the difference between salt
and meat is substantial, and to keep the symmetry of
exchange correct the second man added bread.

To make the most of their combined wealth, the two
prisoners went through a ritual, understood by all, of
"giving, receiving, repaying." Their act is the concentration-camp version of an elementary social institution

which Marcel Mauss has called the "gift relation" or "gift morality." Mauss observes that in societies of an archaic or segmentary nature, gift-giving becomes a medium through which people "are constantly embroiled with and feel themselves in debt to each other" (31). Which is to say that men and women give in expectation of return, and those who receive feel bound to repay. Yet the whole of this process is more instinctive than reasoned upon, and the full power of the gift relation depends finally on an absence of conscious calculation. People give and receive, not to bribe or acquire, but to establish relations. Since the gift is identified with the donor, the act of giving creates a personal tie, and Mauss suggests that "the gift itself constitutes an irrevocable link especially when it is a gift of food" (58).

Gift-giving, in other words, creates bonds at once spiritual and concrete, social and economic. It is one of the ties which bind. Exchange brings people together, and makes them conscious of their worth in each other's eyes. Self-interest turns to goodwill, and the gift relation becomes one of the constitutive structures of social being. Through rituals of exchange the dehumanizing effect of xenophobia and mistrust—everything which keeps us apart and at war—is transformed into trust, acquaintance, respect, conditions which bring men together and allow them to function as units distinct yet in concord, each honoring the other's claim to dignity. The gift transforms hostility into allegiance. Even among animals, as ethologists point out, social bonding is achieved through rituals which suppress or transform aggression: "in fact, this bond is the firmer, the more aggressive the particular animal and species is" (Lorenz, 216). If this is true for animals, and for people in primitive societies, how very important for men and women in the concentration camps, where conditions of deprivation and fear intensified the tendency toward mistrust and anger.

Through giving and sharing the state of potential warfare was transcended. In its place sprang up binding moments of frail but real communion:

> There are days when the chief is not here. He bolts the barracks and leaves complete freedom to the locked-in workers. These are wonderful days. A small bribe changes Inga [the *Kapo*] into an angel, graciously open to any further proofs of friendship. From hiding places pots, saucepans, frying pans appear. Someone has potatoes, somebody else a ration of margarine, another has onions and someone else a spoonful of flour for gravy. . . . On the top of the stove, no larger than twenty square inches, fifty women do their cooking, working in accord and harmony (Szmaglewska, 100).

Whatever form it took, food-sharing was a mode of human interchange through which the survivor's all but defeated humanity could be regained and kept going:

> It became a regular custom in the factory—bearing witness to increased solidarity—that a jug of warm liquid or bread slops passed from hand to hand, among all those at the same work-table. Each woman took a sip, first the sick, then the healthy, by turn. . . . If anyone managed to flavor the water with a pinch of salt acquired somewhere, a scrap of margarine, or clove of garlic, all her comrades without exception enjoyed it. This was a good custom, a humane custom, even though the conditions

of our lives were becoming increasingly bestial (Birenbaum, 147).

It was more than a custom; it was, and is, one of the structures of humanness.

"Gift morality" did not, of course, issue in an articulated system of ethics among prisoners. It remained implicit in concrete acts and relations. But in one all-important way a kind of morality did become conscious. In all the camps, Soviet and Nazi alike, there was one law and one law only which all prisoners knew and accepted. This was the "bread law," as it came to be called. And in a definite and clear-cut sense this particular "law" was the foundation and focal point of moral order in the concentration camps. A survivor of Sachsenhausen describes its origin and enforcement:

Thefts occurred continually in the prisoners' barracks, ours as well as others. Hunger tormented us all incessantly and transformed men into irresponsible beasts. Even those who had formerly passed for honorable men stole from their comrades the bits of bread that many had laid by from their evening ration for the next day. By day, all with one voice condemned the theft. By night, the stealing was repeated, just the same. In our conversation periods we sought counter-measures. We knew that the thieves did not realize the crime they were committing, for hunger had driven them nearly out of their senses. But we knew also that these bits of bread were the life-preserver by which we might keep ourselves afloat until the longed-for moment of freedom. And when we caught a bread thief, we punished him so severely that he lost his taste for stealing (Szalet, 152).

A survivor of the Soviet camps describes the same situation:

> The theft of bread among the prisoners themselves was, alas, not altogether rare. Theft from a comrade, no matter in what form, was the most serious crime (next to being an informer) that a prisoner could commit. The punishment meted out by the thief's own comrades was correspondingly harsh (Nork, 56).

It could be harsh indeed, as when a bread thief was caught in an Auschwitz barracks:

> "So what happened? Did the others beat him up?"
> "They killed him, of course. What's the use of beating up a bastard like that?"
> That was the law in Block 18. If a man stole your food, you killed him. If you were not strong enough to carry out the sentence yourself, there were other executioners; it was rough justice, but it was fair because to deprive a man of food was to murder (Vrba, 115).

Hard as such measures seem, an inflexible enforcement of the bread law was necessary, and not just to protect the individual, but to preserve a basis of trust and community on which everyone's life and humanness depended:

> I saw people grow pale and collapse when they realized that their piece of bread had been stolen. And it was not only a wrong that had been done to them directly. It was an irreparable wrong that

had been done to all of us. For suspicion settled in,
and distrust and hate (Semprun, 60).

The difference between anomie and order, between
the sense that nothing mattered and the feeling that
even in such places a faintly discerned goodness existed,
actually rested on the bread law. It was vital to everyone because theft undermined the significance of giving
and receiving, and thereby wrecked the exceedingly frail
fabric of social existence as a whole. A survivor of
Buchenwald sums it up:

> If hunger so demoralized a man that he stole an-
> other's bread, no one reported him to the SS or
> even to the Block Leader. The room attendants
> themselves took care of him. . . . If he did not die
> of the beating, they so incapacitated him that he
> was fit only for the crematorium. . . . [We] ap-
> proved of this rule because it actually helped us
> maintain a certain standard of morale and mutual
> trust (Weinstock, 120-21).

The assumption that there was no moral or social order
in the concentration camps is wrong. Except peripheral-
ly and for brief periods similar to the "initial collapse"
of individuals, the general condition we call chaos or
anomie—what philosophers designate as the "state of
nature"—did not exist. Certainly it did not prevail.
Through innumerable small acts of humanness, most of
them covert but everywhere in evidence, survivors were
able to maintain societal structures workable enough to
keep themselves alive and morally sane. The "state of
nature," it turns out, is not natural. A war of all against
all must be imposed by force, and no sooner has it

started than those who suffer it begin, spontaneously and without plan, to transcend it.

The "state of nature" is a vacuum which nature itself abhors, an observation made in 1651 by Thomas Hobbes, who defined it as "that condition which is called war, and such a war as is of every man against every man" (106). He goes on to argue that although chaos exists in potential, it does not occur in fact, and for this reason: "nature" provides "laws," knowable through reason, "which tend to nature's preservation" (130). These "laws of nature," in Hobbes' view, are the constituents of existence itself—conditions which come into being and flourish. If chaos were absolute, there would be neither the time nor the peace necessary for man's fundamental activities:

> . . . no culture of the earth . . . no commodious
> building . . . no account of time . . . no society;
> and, which is worst of all, continual fear and
> danger of violent death; and the life of man soli-
> tary, poor, nasty, brutish, and short (107).

Hobbes' aim, in *Leviathan,* was to rationalize force and provide a naturalistic basis for ethics. He wished to define government as a power dedicated to the life and well-being of the community through enforcement of an order based on nature's laws. His principal assumption is that life or nature *protects itself* through forms of necessary behavior which are at once natural and human. Hobbes was thus a forerunner of the Enlightenment in arguing that even the moral law is but a finer version of nature's law. His hope as a social philosopher was to find cause in nature itself for the ethical imperatives on which social harmony and fruitful life depend. He would have agreed that the survivor's behavior is inherently moral, and *must* be, since over time conditions of amoral struggle destroy not only the possibility of human fulfillment, but finally the fabric of existence itself. He was mistaken in one thing only, for like the Enlightenment thinkers to follow him, he assumed that the natural order is a rational order.

Morality and society do not rest on reason, although the critique of them does. But certainly they rest on something, and something too which, in a stricter sense than Hobbes could have known, deserves the name *nature*. The biological sciences confirm the fact that all life depends on systems, that everywhere a tendency to order governs behavior. From cells to men, life-forms possess both internal and external means of bonding and communication. Social behavior among higher animals is very pronounced, having evolved through a process of natural selection to the present range of structures, all of which serve the cause of survival. We are beginning to understand, in other words, that "man comes to sociability not by arrangement, by rational decision, but from the natural primary disposition which he shares with all other higher animals" (Portman, 70). Social organization is a function of life itself, and in man it reaches a pitch of interrelatedness and mutual recognition which in fact constitutes, or is the prior condition for, humanness as we know it.

Hobbes was right in his way. Nature itself—by which I mean the system of living creatures—guards against dissolution and chaos; not through control by government, nor even by rational adherence to "laws of nature," but through the emergence, during times of prolonged crisis, of structures of behavior whose purpose is to maintain the social basis of life. Order emerges. That, as biologists like to observe, is the first and most striking fact about life, since entropy or the tendency to dissolution characterizes all inorganic kinds of organization. For survivors this is crucial. Uprooted and flung into chaos, they do what they must to stay alive, and in that doing achieve enough society to meet the crisis humanly, together. After the period of initial collapse comes reintegration, a process which usually occurs gradually, in accord with the fact that all things human take time. In some cases, however, it can happen remarkably fast, as in the following example from the ordeal of mass deportation:

> Ninety-six persons had been thrust into our car, including many children who were squeezed in among the luggage. . . . As the first hour and then the second passed, we perceived that the simplest details of existence would be extremely complicated. Sanitary disposal was out of the question. . . . As the journey stretched endlessly, the car jerking and jolting, all the forces of nature conspired against us ninety-six. A torrid sun heated the walls until the air became suffocating. . . . The travelers were mostly persons of culture and position from our community. . . . But as the hours slipped away the veneers cracked. Soon there were incidents and, later, serious quarrels. . . . The children cried; the sick groaned; the old people lamented. . . . As night fell we lost all concept of human behavior and the wrangling increased until the car was a bedlam. . . . Finally, the cooler heads prevailed and a semblance of order was restored. A doctor and I were chosen captains-in-charge (Lengyel, 6-7).

The "veneer" of cultivated behavior, which served well enough in normal times, was not equal to such stress. Fear and panic were the initial response, and for a time all was chaos. But then, as necessity bore down and hysteria gave way to realism, a more elementary kind of order, or at least a readiness, began to function. A condition came into being which allowed the "cooler heads" to be heard. Amid this mess they held an election, they came to agree on basic responsibilities, and settled down to face their common plight. This achievement may have been but a "semblance" of past order, but it was sufficient to keep the ninety-six people in that boxcar sane and alive and above the threshold of brutality.

From the last days of the Warsaw Ghetto, when the SS was systematically hunting down everyone, comes another example. Those who remained took refuge in cellars, in attics, behind false walls where they waited:

The bunker grew increasingly crowded and stuffy. Anyone who went to the water-tap or toilet collided with others or stumbled over their neighbors in the darkness. There was no end to the disputes and squabbles, fights over nothing, insults, name-calling. Exhausted by the want of fresh air and the most elementary facilities, tortured by incessant fear and uncertainty, people began losing their self-control. The bunker became a real hell. . . . Yet, in the midst of this suffering, there grew up a solidarity, a mutual understanding and sympathy. It was no longer necessary to shout for quiet, lest the SS track us down, nor ask too long for neighborly help. People helped one another, even shared the last drops of medicine, without caring whether someone was a relative or a stranger, a friend or unknown, poor or rich. The differences between us disappeared. In the end, our mutual and tragic fate had united us into one great family (Birenbaum, 71-75).

Civility disintegrates and disorder prevails. Then slowly, in sorrow and a realism never before faced up to, the mass of flailing people grow quiet and neighborly, and in the end rest almost peaceful in primitive communion. In this and other instances,

> . . . the simple, shapeless agglomeration of human beings assembled by chance reveals a hidden structure of available wills, an astonishing plasticity which takes shape according to certain lines of force, reveals plans and projects which are perhaps unfeasible but which lend a meaning, a coherence to even the most absurd, the most desperate of human acts (Semprun, 205).

Order emerges, people turn to one another in "neighborly help." This pattern was everywhere apparent in the world of the camps. Giving and receiving were perpetual, and we can only imagine the intensity of such transactions. When men and women know they are dying, smallest favors can shake the frail world of their being with seismic force. The power of such moments is enormous, and the bonds thus created go far deeper than guilt or pride or ordinary obligation. And perhaps the most striking thing about this kind of giving, apart from the extreme gratitude it could generate, is the fact that pity played no part:

> Yet, how little sometimes suffices to save a perishing man: a glance, a word, a gesture. Once I gave a fellow prisoner a boiled potato and he never stopped thanking me for having saved his life. An-

other time I helped someone to regain his feet after he had fallen during a march. He not only reached our destination alive, but survived the war; and he maintains that without my help that one time he would never have gotten up, he would have been killed where he lay. In the camp it was easier to get a piece of bread than a kind word. Prisoners helped one another as best they could, but they shied away from sentiment. Help, yes, compassion, no (Donat, 237).

Compassion means to "suffer with." It is an act of imaginative entrance into the world of another's pain, and is proper on the part of those who do not themselves bear the same kind or degree of suffering. Through compassion we close the distance between one condition and another, and as long as the division between unearned luck and unearned disaster remains a structure of our common world, compassion has about it the nature of a moral imperative. But only for us, whom fate has not tried. For survivors it was different: "Everyone in camp had lost someone and all bore their grief in silence. Another's tears met with understanding, but not with sympathy: one unhappy man doesn't pity another, is not moved by another's misfortune" (Donat, 237). Or as one woman said to another:

"Why do you cry?" . . . I sobbed even harder. . . . "Really, why do you cry? . . . We are all here together; we all have it as hard" (Pawlowicz, 113).

The survivor's behavior is not inspired by pity, nor can it be explained in terms of reason alone. Underground resistance groups were guided by rational assessment of the situation being faced, and through time most survivors developed a degree of political consciousness, an awareness of the common predicament and of the need to act collectively. But what came first was spontaneous involvement in each other's lives on the immediate level of giving and receiving. And like the need to bear witness, which might also be viewed rationally, there was yet an instinctive depth to the emergence of social order through help and sharing. Human interchange goes on all the time everywhere. But in the concentration camps it was more naked, more urgently pursued. Judging from the experience of survivors, "gift morality" and a will to communion are constitutive elements of humanness. In extremity, behavior of this kind emerges without plan or instruction, simply as the means to life.

VI

US AND THEM

All around and beneath her she could hear strange submerged sounds, groaning, choking and sobbing: many of the people were not dead yet. The whole mass of bodies kept moving slightly as they settled down and were pressed tighter by the movements of the ones who were still alive. . . . Then she heard people walking near her, actually on the bodies . . . , occasionally firing at those which showed signs of life. . . . One SS man . . . shone his torch on her, . . . but she . . . gave no signs of life.

A. KUZNETSOV
Babi Yar

That corpse you planted last year in
    your garden,
Has it begun to sprout? Will it bloom
    this year?
Or has the sudden frost disturbed
    its bed?

T. S. ELIOT
The Waste Land

IN 1959 Stanley M. Elkins put forward his slave-as-sambo thesis in *Slavery,* arguing that the personality of the American slave had been fundamentally regressive and infantile. Elkins does not examine direct evidence; he uses a "comparative" method, and his main comparison is with inmates of the German concentration camps. To identify the Southern plantation with Auschwitz is senseless, of course; but the comparison is still significant, not for what it tells us of either slaves or survivors, but for the assumptions that are made about behavior in extremity. Elkins takes it for granted that in the camps men and women lost their capacity to act as morally responsible adults, and the point of his comparison is to demonstrate that this also happened to American slaves. Specifically, he states that "old prisoners," by which he means the survivors, suffered "deep disintegrative effects" (107); that the "most immediate aspect of the old inmates' behavior . . . was its *childlike* quality" (111); and finally that "all" survivors were "reduced to complete and childish dependence upon their masters" (113). Elkins goes on to say that regression began with the abandonment of previous ethical standards, and to make his point he quotes as representative a brief statement by a survivor of Auschwitz. In Elkins' context, here is her remark:

One part of the prisoner's being was thus, under sharp stress, brought to the crude realization that he must thenceforth be governed by an entire new set of standards in order to live. Mrs. Lingens-Reiner puts it bluntly: "Will you survive or shall I? As soon as one sensed that this was at stake everyone turned egotist" (109-10).

In extremity, in other words, everyone fights alone; and the "entire new set of standards" comes from the camp system itself. But is there not a contradiction here? Childlike behavior is not the same as rapacious battle in one's best self-interest. The former entails passivity and preference for illusion; the latter demands intelligent calculation and a capacity for quick, objective judgment. All the same, that survivors suffered regression to infantile stages, *and* that they were amoral monsters, are very widespread notions. They constitute nothing less than the prevailing view of survival behavior. Not surprisingly, in *Death in Life* Robert Lifton has used the same quotation—"Will you survive, or shall I?"—as a representative expression of the "competition for survival" which, in his view, lies at the root of the "guilt" survivors are supposed to feel (490). What, then, are we to make of the Lingens-Reiner statement? Is it a fair summation of her own view?

In *Prisoners of Fear* she aims to tell the very worst; and the most striking thing about her testimony is the double vision we have already noted in reports by survivors. The viciousness and horror are certainly there, but also examples of morally intelligent behavior, and many references to resistance and solidarity among camp inmates. There is the moment when the narrator exposes herself by taking action to get another prisoner's

name off a death list. She does this, all the time calling
herself a fool for taking the risk, because she sees an
opportunity: there was a *way* to save someone and that
decided her. The incident takes four pages to describe
(79-82) and is not an example of "survival egotism" or
of "infantile regression." It is one instance among many
of men and women acting with courage and intelligence
to help others. The following are typical:

> There were girls among them who lived through a
> typhus attack without staying in bed. Two of their
> friends would take the sick comrade between them,
> when she had a temperature of 103° F. and saw
> everything as a blur, and drag her along with their
> labour gang; out in the fields they would lay her
> down under a shrub, and in the evening they would
> march her back to camp—all to avoid her being
> sent to the hospital hut and so being exposed to
> the danger of a selection (122).

> The camp doctor would line up all the Jewish pa-
> tients. . . . All those who were too ill to get out of
> bed were lost from the outset. . . . The rest of the
> prisoners did everything in their power to obstruct
> the doctor and to save one or other of the victims;
> I do not think that a single one among us withheld
> her help. We would hide women somewhere in the
> hut. . . . We would smuggle them into "Aryan"
> huts. . . . We would put their names on the list of
> patients due for release (76-7).

> Under the pressure of a concentration camp you
> grew more closely attached to people than you
> would have done otherwise in such a short time
> (162).

The pursuit of self-interest was certainly a determinant of behavior in the camps, but it was everywhere countered by an unsuppressible urge toward decency and care, a multitude of small deeds against the grain of one's "best" interest. Prisoners looked out for themselves first of all, but also for one another when and however they could. In the whole body of testimony by survivors there is no better description of this contradiction than in the book by Lingens-Reiner:

Ena Weiss, our Chief Doctor—one of the most intelligent, gifted and eminent Jewish women in the camp—once defined her attitude thus, in sarcastic rejection of fulsome flattery and at the same time with brutal frankness: "How did I keep alive in Auschwitz? My principle is: myself first, second and third. Then nothing. Then myself again—and then all the others." This formula expressed the only principle which was possible for Jews who intended—almost insanely intended—to survive Auschwitz. Yet, because this woman had the icy wisdom and strength to accept the principle, she kept for herself a position in which she could do something for the Jews. Hardly anybody else in the camp did as much for them and saved so many lives as she did (118).

At least in this instance, Elkins' thesis is not borne out by the evidence from which he quotes, and if for a time his "sambo" theory of slave behavior was accepted, that was not because he had offered solid evidence but because by comparing slavery to the camp experience he was able to mobilize the deeply disturbing and largely uncontrolled range of reaction which attends our idea of the concentration camps. Here is how he sums it up:

Daily life in the camp, with its fear and tensions, taught over and over the lesson of absolute power. It prepared the personality for a drastic shift in standards. It crushed whatever anxieties might have been drawn from prior standards; such standards had become meaningless. It focused the prisoner's attention constantly on the moods, attitudes, and standards of the only man who mattered [the SS guard]. A truly childlike situation was thus created: utter and abject dependency. . . . It is thus no wonder that the prisoners should become "as children." It is no wonder that their obedience became unquestioning, that they did not revolt, that they could not "hate" their masters (122).

Elkins is simply reiterating accepted ideas. But power is never absolute, especially over time, and it is not true that the SS guard was the "one significant other" on whom the prisoners' needs depended. Social bonding among prisoners themselves was a universal phenomenon in the camps. And of course it is not true that survivors were morally crushed, that they lost all sense of prior standards, that moral sanity was meaningless. Certainly it is not true that they did not revolt; to live was to resist, every day, all the time, and in addition to dramatic events like the burning of Treblinka and Sobibor there were many small revolts in which all perished. Prisoners who were capable, furthermore, of organizing an underground and of systematically subverting SS intentions were not behaving "as children." And it is not true, finally, that hatred was absent. Survivors seethed with it, they speak of it often, they describe terrible acts of revenge. In *Prisoners of Fear* the author praises one of her comrades for "the ice-cold self-control by which she hid her abysmal hatred of the German rulers" (123) in order to exploit them.

Ella Lingens-Reiner's own rage rings through her prose on every page.

No, most of this was not true, not for many survivors in many camps. Hence these disturbing questions: Why do we insist that prisoners died "like sheep"? Why is it easy to believe, despite the contradiction, that survivors were infantile *and* that they were cunning manipulators using every kind of betrayal and base trick to stay alive? Why, in short, do we insist that survivors did not really survive: that they suffered "death in life" and that if they are alive in body their spirit was destroyed beyond salvaging? Here is how one psychoanalytic commentator summed up the opinions of his colleagues in a symposium on the camp experience: "To one degree or another, they all stifled their true feelings, they all denied the dictates of conscience and social feeling in hope of survival, and they were all warped and distorted as a result" (Hoppe, 83). That word "all"—its assurance, its contempt—must be accounted for.

To date, serious study of the concentration-camp experience has been done almost exclusively from the psychoanalytic point of view. Elkins takes the bulk of his evidence from Elie Cohen and Bruno Bettelheim, both of whom employ the psychoanalytic approach, both of whom offer much valuable insight, but both of whom, in the end, are led by their method to mistaken conclusions. The psychoanalytic approach is misleading because it is essentially a theory of culture and of man in the civilized state. Its analytic power—which is considerable—is maximized when turned upon behavior which is symbolic, mediated, and therefore at a sufficient remove from necessity. To be of use, the psychoanalytic method, which is that of interpretation, must be applied to actions which have more than one meaning *on the level of meaning*. But that is not the case with extremity. When men and women must respond directly to necessity—when defilement occurs at gun-point and the most undelayable of needs determines action, or when death itself is the determinant—then behavior has no "meaning" at all in a symbolic or psychological sense.

The purpose of action in extremity is to keep life going; the multiplicity of motive which gives civilized behavior its depth and complexity is lost. We have seen that life in the camps depended on a duality of behavior, but this duality—this layering of behavior—is very different from the kind of layering which psychoanalysis probes. In extremity, action splits into "primary" and "secondary" levels of adjustment, each of which is real and separate in itself. Precisely here the psychoanalytic approach misleads us: in its search for a second meaning on the first or primary level, it overlooks the secondary level. For psychoanalysis, covert behavior is implicit behavior. But for survivors it becomes explicit, actual, necessary in an immediately practical way.

I am assuming, with Freud, that the phenomenon of civilization, no matter how advanced or primitive, is based first of all on processes of sublimation and symbolization. Taken in this broad sense, civilization as a condition can be described as the transcendence of primal needs and crude necessities through systems of technical and symbolic mediation. Thereby a realm of freedom comes into being which is not governed immediately by the necessities which constitute extremity. Prisoners in a concentration camp would eat anything, at any time they could get it, in almost any state of rawness or decay. We, on the other hand, eat the kind of food we choose, when we choose, after it has been transformed aesthetically through cooking, and upon occasions rich in ritual observance. And thus too, the dead in the camps were stacked naked in piles, rammed into ovens, tossed every which way into ditches and pits. But the man or woman who dies in normal circumstances becomes the object of complicated ritual procedures which confer meaning and dignity upon his or her death and thereby humanize it. The primacy of death is denied symbolically, the immediate facts are overlaid with solemn meaning and removed from the center of consciousness. Death is no longer *thought of* as death, just as animal flesh is no longer thought of as animal flesh after it has been transformed by cooking and table rites.

Freedom to mediate facts and instill new significance, to create and multiply meanings, is the essence of civilization. And here the psychoanalytic method correctly assumes that nothing is to be taken at face value. Our actions are invested with memories, wishes and values reaching far beyond the performance itself, and no act is simply and wholly significant in its immediate, concrete function. Historically, psychoanalysis originated just as the *symboliste* movement was occurring in the arts, and it is tempting to see in both a common pursuit. Both read facts as symbols, both search out the mysteries of an invisible drama, and both take it for granted that in any act or situation there is more than meets the eye. Survivors act as they do because they must—the issue is always life or death—and at every moment the meaning and purpose of their behavior is fully known. We, on the other hand, act for all kinds of reasons, some known and others unconscious, some practical and others governed by an internal will that can only be guessed at. For us behavior requires interpretation; indeed, interpretation validates experience, and hence the usefulness of the psychoanalytic approach.

But only for us. Attempts to interpret the survivor's experience—to see it in terms other than its own—have done more harm than good. The outstanding spokesman, in this respect, has been Bruno Bettelheim, whose application of the psychoanalytic model to survival behavior has been definitive. Bettelheim was in Buchenwald and Dachau for a year, at a time when prisoners could still hope for release, and before systematic destruction became fixed policy, but he was there and speaks with that authority. His first analysis of the camp experience—"Individual and Mass Behavior in Extreme Situations"—appeared in 1943, adding the weight of precedence to a position which has never been challenged and which has influenced all subsequent study. Even among laymen his ideas are known and accepted. His version is *the* version, and in *The Informed Heart* it takes its final, polemical form. Bettelheim argues that prisoners in the camps exhibited the following general traits: they became "incompetent children"; they identified with the SS, "willing and able to accept SS values and behavior"; they fell into an "anonymous mass," without social base or organization; and they possessed no "autonomy," by which he means the capacity for dramatic acts of self-assertion.

Bettelheim's view differs sharply from that of other survivors—Ernst Wiechert and Ernest Rappaport, for example—who were in Buchenwald at the same time. His claims are not substantiated in the bulk of testimony by survivors, including the comprehensive report by Eugen Kogon, who was a member of the underground and was in Buchenwald from the beginning to the end. Bettelheim's attack on Anne Frank and her family is perhaps the essential expression of his outlook. He suggests that their decision to stay together and go into hiding was stupid—a judgment which disregards the situation in Holland, where the population at large helped many Jews to escape in this way. Rather, he argues, they should have abandoned their commitment to each other: each should have fought alone, each shooting down the Germans as they came. Where the guns were to come from, or how scattered individuals were to succeed when nations failed, he does not say.

Bettelheim develops his argument in terms of a dramatic contrast between the individual, who possesses "autonomy," and the masses, who do not possess "autonomy." In many cases this becomes a contrast between Bettelheim himself and "others":

> They appeared to be pathological liars, were unable to restrain themselves, unable to separate clearly between reality and their wishful or anxious daydreams. So to the old worries, a new one was added, namely, "How could I protect myself from becoming as they are?" (114).

This may refer to prisoners during the stage of initial collapse, but Bettelheim does not say so. He is describing what appears to him to be the general situation, and this contrast between himself and other prisoners is in fact the theme of his book. It is evident not only in the sense of isolation and superiority which attends references to himself, but also in an animus toward other prisoners generally. At one point he attacks camp functionaries by suggesting that inmates with "privileged" positions had "a greater need to justify themselves":

> This they did as members of ruling classes for centuries have done—by pointing to their greater

value to society because of their power to influence,
their education, their cultural refinement (186).

His specific example is Eugen Kogon:

> Kogon's attitudes are fairly representative. For
> example, he took pride that in the stillness of the
> night he enjoyed reading Plato or Galsworthy,
> while in an adjacent room the air reeked of com-
> mon prisoners, while they snored unpleasantly. He
> seemed unable to realize that only his privileged
> position, based on participation in human experi-
> ments, gave him the leisure to enjoy culture, an
> enjoyment he then used to justify his privileged
> position (186).

That sounds convincing, but let us look at Kogon's
description of the same event:

> In the winter of 1942-43 a succession of bread
> thefts in Barracks 42 at Buchenwald made it neces-
> sary to establish a nightwatch. For months on end
> I volunteered for this duty, taking the shift from
> three to six o'clock in the morning. It meant sitting
> alone in the day room, while the snores of the com-
> rades came from the other end. For once I was
> free of the ineluctable companionship that usually
> shackled and stifled every individual activity. What
> an experience it was to sit quietly by a shaded
> lamp, delving into the pages of Plato's *Dialogues,*
> Galsworthy's *Swan Song,* or the works of Heine,
> Klabund, Mehring! (132).

One of the anomalies of Nazi rule was that books unobtainable in the whole of the Reich were available in

the camps. Kogon goes on: "Yes, they could be read illegally in camp. They were among books retrieved from the nation-wide wastepaper collections. The Nazis impounded many libraries of 'enemies of the state,' and turned them over to these collections" (132). There is perhaps a sense of amusement in Kogon's recounting of such details—a *Swan Song* in Buchenwald?—but not a trace of what Bettelheim calls the "need to justify."

Kogon's book, *The Theory and Practice of Hell,* is an extensive record of the achievements of the political underground in Buchenwald, including methods of organization, strategic use of functionary positions, and a detailed account of the take-over of the camp by the prisoners. The episode Bettelheim singles out is, in Kogon's view, just another small example of resistance in action. As a member of the underground, Kogon is simply doing his job. The reason he is there is not to read Plato and Mehring, but to enforce the bread law and thereby help keep a sense of moral order alive among the prisoners. He does not, as Bettelheim says, refer to air which "reeked of common prisoners," but to his "comrades." His private enjoyment is a by-product of responsibility, and if there had been no books Kogon would have volunteered all the same, going without sufficient sleep "for months on end" to do his duty as a man committed to the general struggle.

Bettelheim did not know Kogon in camp, and the incident cited above (one of several he takes from Kogon's report) occurred after his release. Yet this is not a matter of ignorance merely. To reduce Kogon's act to "privilege," and further to declare that it was "based on participation in human experiments," is a grave misrepresentation of basic facts. Bettelheim's obsession with "autonomy," his concept of transcendental selfhood, blinds him to collective action and mutual aid. After reading Kogon's book he remains unaware of organized resistance and of the enormous benefits which the camp population received through covert operations of the underground. He goes on to criticize prisoners who did not, at some point, assert their "autonomy" by openly risking their lives (Kogon's was on the line for nine years but never, if he could help it, openly). Bettelheim tells us that the act he himself performed by talking back to an SS officer, thereby risking his life in a dramatic assertion of self, was the kind of behavior all survivors should have displayed. And that is the heart of the matter. Bettelheim's critique of camp behavior is rooted in the old heroic ethic. Heroism, for him, is an isolated act of defiance through which the individual *as* an individual confronts death. Bettelheim's position is clear from the kind of action he praises:

Once, a group of naked prisoners about to enter the gas chamber stood lined up in front of it. In some way the commanding SS officer learned that one of the women prisoners had been a dancer. So he ordered her to dance for him. She did, and as she danced, she approached him, seized his gun, and shot him down. She too was immediately shot to death (264-65).

"She was willing to risk her life," Bettelheim concludes, "to achieve autonomy once more" (265). But this is not an example of risking life. The act he celebrates is suicide. It is courageous, beautiful, and under the circumstances the only alternative to passive surrender. It is heroic, but it is still suicide. What can "autonomy" at the cost of personal destruction amount to? How effective would underground activities, or any of the forms of resistance, have been on such a principle? Bettelheim's argument comes down to this: "manhood" requires dramatic self-confirmation, and in the camps this could only be achieved through some moment of open confrontation with death. Insofar as the struggle for life did not become overtly rebellious, prisoners were "childlike."

Bettelheim's polemical objective, in *The Informed Heart,* is to compare the survivor's experience with the predicament of modern man in "mass society," in order to arrive at a critique of the latter. The comparison itself is invalid. No matter how disconcerting conditions become for us, they do not hinge at every moment on the issue of life and death; pain is not constant, options abound, the rule of terror and necessity is far from total. Life for us does not depend on collective action— not directly, that is; nor is death the price of visibility. Bettelheim wishes to rouse us from our sense of victimhood; but by claiming that pressure reduces men and women to children, and by praising a heroism based on death, he tends instead to support what he fears.

Whatever his conclusions, Bettelheim's argument for "autonomy" is a defense of human dignity, a call to that principle in man which resists determination by otherness. His fear is not only that human beings can be made helpless, but that prevailing tendencies in modern thinking have accepted the condition of victimhood as final. A primary assumption of his own discipline is that the self is forever in painful bondage to its past. And much of social, economic and political theory— conservative as well as radical—takes it for granted that external forces shape internal being, or finally that the self is constituted by forces it neither controls nor understands but only suffers. Perhaps the case for man-as-victim has been put most strongly by behaviorism, which assumes outright that environment is omnipotent and that the human self is ever and always a unilateral function of the world in which it finds itself. Applied to the concentration camps, the conclusion can only be that monstrosity breeds monstrosity, and therefore that no one survived. Those not killed in body most surely perished in spirit, for men and women could not long endure such inhumanity without themselves becoming inhuman. One sees why B. F. Skinner, in his attack on freedom, also finds it necessary to attack dignity: as long as people persist in their refusal to be determined by forces external to themselves, the belief in freedom will likewise persist as a by-product of this basic recalcitrance.

That the concentration camps were a kind of "experiment" has often been noted. Their aim was to reduce inmates to mindless creatures whose behavior could be predicted and controlled absolutely. The camps have so far been the closest thing on earth to a perfect Skinner Box. They were a closed, completely regulated environment, a "total" world in the strict sense. Pain and death were the "negative reinforcers," food and life the "positive reinforcers," and all these forces were pulling and shoving twenty-four hours a day at the deepest stratum of human need. And yet, survivors are proof that the "experiment" did not succeed.

Their behavior was of course determined by camp conditions, but not in the way behaviorism or current theories of victimhood assume. The distinction overlooked is between responses to necessity which are really unilateral and therefore at one with necessity, and responses which are strategic and therefore provoked by, but opposed to, the same necessity. Facing extreme pressure, human beings either acquiesce or resist or do both. Like the psychoanalytic approach, behaviorism does not take into account the duality of action in extremity. It too fixes attention on the "primary" level of adjustment, precisely on those activities which are informed by, and expressive of, camp logic. On this level it appears that prisoners succumbed to their environment (and life depended on the success of this deception). But on the "secondary" level, as we have seen, prisoners were pushing hard against camp controls. And it is perhaps worth noting, finally, that the behaviorist assumption was held in practice by the SS themselves, who never doubted that force and fear could break anyone, could reduce all behavior to a function of their world.

In a way at first surprising, Bettelheim's idea of heroism dovetails with the view of man as victim—just as psychoanalysis and behaviorism, based on opposite principles, agree in the case of extremity. But in fact, the celebration of man's "indomitable spirit" and our acceptance of victimhood are rooted in the single belief, as old as Western culture, that human bondage can be transcended only in death. Death is at once the entrance to a world of fulfillment unobtainable on earth and the proof of a spirit unvanquished by fear or compromise. Neither is possible to men and women getting by as best they can from day to day; and a life not ready, at any moment, to give itself for something higher is life enchained, life cowed and disgraced by its own gross will to persist. Survival in itself, not dedicated to something else, has never been held in high esteem and often has been viewed with contempt. This complex of attitudes is at the heart of the Christian worldview; it had already been expounded in detail by Plato, and before that invested with grandeur by Homer. In the *Iliad,* the progress of a Greek advance is stopped by sudden mist and darkness; whereupon the great Ajax prays aloud for Zeus to send light to continue the battle, even if light should bring death. Many centuries later, in *On the Sublime,* Longinus remarked: "That is the true attitude of an Ajax. He does not pray for life, for such a petition would have ill beseemed a hero" (67).

Just so; when we say of someone that he or she "merely" survives, the word "merely" carries real if muted moral objection. And we say it all the time, as if to be alive, or simply to struggle for life, were not in itself enough. For "meaning" and "significance" we look elsewhere—to ideals and ideologies, to religion and other metaphysical systems; to anything, any *higher* cause or goal which defines life in terms other than its own and thereby justifies existence. Survivors are suspect because they are forced to do openly, without a shred of style or fine language to cover themselves, what the rest of us do by remote control. The bias against "mere survival" runs deep, and derives its force from the fact that all of us think and act in terms of survival, but at a crucial remove and with all the masks and stratagems which cultivated men and women learn to use—of which there would seem to be no end. As Nietzsche observed, man would rather will nothingness than have nothing to will, nothing with which to push life beyond itself. But as Nietzsche implies, the problem with these symbolic superstructures is that they redeem life by negating it.

One of the side-effects of civilization is that life is enhanced by denigrating actual life processes. But is this a side-effect merely? Might it not be the paradox of civilization itself—a direct result of, or even a condition for, the split between mind and body which characterizes the structure of civilized existence as we know it? Surely Descartes was not original when he declared that mind and matter are separate entities, nor was his "I think therefore I am" anything more than the commonplace bias of culture itself. Within the framework of civilization, experience has always been divided into physical and spiritual realms, immediate and mediated modes, concrete and symbolic forms, lower and higher activities. And all things "higher," as we know, are by definition *not* concerned with life itself; not, that is, with life in its physical concreteness.

In *The Presentation of Self in Everyday Life* Erving Goffman has observed that human activities take place either in "front" or in "back" regions. We "present" ourselves (our idealized selves) to ourselves and others in "front regions," while keeping our props, especially those which attend our biological needs, out of sight in "back regions":

> The line dividing front and back regions is illustrated everywhere in our society. As suggested, the bathroom and bedroom . . . are places from which the downstairs audience can be excluded. Bodies that are cleansed, clothed, and made up in these rooms can be presented to friends in others. In the kitchen, of course, there is done to food what in the bathroom and bedroom is done to the human body (123).

Goffman is talking about American society, but the compartmentalization of existence to which he points can be found everywhere, most dramatically at events which have a religious or an official function, places and ceremonies associated with power or the sacred. In all such instances, a division between front and back, higher and lower, is strictly upheld. And as far as ritual and technology permit, everything "lower" is kept out of sight—and thereby out of mind. Mary Douglas has called this "the purity rule":

> According to the rule of distance from physiological origin (or the purity rule) the more the social situation exerts pressure on persons involved in it, the more the social demand for conformity tends to be expressed by a demand for physical control. Bodily processes are more ignored and more firmly set outside the social discourse, the more the latter is important. A natural way of investing a social occasion with dignity is to hide organic processes (12).

The division between body and mind, between lower and higher, is a structural component of civilization as such. Freud's concept of sublimation is helpful here; it refers to the process through which immediate bodily needs are delayed, set at a distance or denied, and finally transformed into the "higher" accomplishments of mind and culture. That which *is* is negated in pursuit of that which *will* be or *should* be. Taken to its religious extreme, this principle results in the negation of this life in favor of another life, higher, purer, elsewhere. Actual existence is "death," whereas death becomes the entrance to "life," or so St. Paul would have us believe. The meaning of life is found *in* death, and the greatest action an individual can perform is to give his life for some "higher" cause.

The trouble with survivors, in our eyes, is that they do not live by the rules. Their needs cannot be delayed, cannot be transformed or got out of sight. Nor do they seek ideal justification for their struggle. Survivors fight merely to live, certain that what counts is life and the

sharing of life. And through this experience of radical
de-sublimation they come, as Nadezhda Mandelstam
puts it, very "close to earth":

> Our way of life kept us firmly rooted to the ground,
> and was not conducive to the search for transcen-
> dental truths. Whenever I talked of suicide, M.
> used to say: "Why hurry? The end is the same
> everywhere, and here they even hasten it for you."
> Death was so much more real, so much simpler
> than life, that we all involuntarily tried to prolong
> our earthly existence, even if only for a brief mo-
> ment—just in case the next day brought some
> relief! In war, in the camps and during periods of
> terror, people think much less about death (let
> alone suicide) than when they are living normal
> lives. Whenever at some point on earth mortal
> terror and the presence of utterly insoluble prob-
> lems are present in a particularly intense form,
> general questions about the nature of being recede
> into the background. . . . In a strange way, despite
> the horror of it, this also gave a certain richness to
> our lives. Who knows what happiness is? Perhaps
> it is better to talk in more concrete terms of the
> fullness or intensity of existence, and in this sense
> there may have been something more deeply satis-
> fying in our desperate clinging to life than in what
> people generally strive for (261).

For years the Mandelstams lived at life's edge: they
saw the tree in winter outline, barren against a barren
land, and saw the strength of its shape. David Rousset,
who passed through several Nazi camps, likewise insists
upon a "positive side" to the experience of survival:

Dynamic awareness of the strength and beauty of the sheer fact of living, in itself, brutal, entirely stripped of all superstructures—living through even the worst of cataclysms and most disastrous setbacks. A cool, sensual thrill of joy founded on the most complete understanding of the wreckage, and consequently incisiveness in action and firmness in decisions, in short, a broader and more intensely creative vigor (171).

Certainly one does not have to survive the concentration camps in order to arrive at awareness of life's immanent value. It can come abruptly, with the shock of death-encounter, or gradually after passing through a period of protracted death-threat, and sometimes in a moment of character-changing revelation. Dostoevsky is a wonderful example. As a young man he was arrested for mildly revolutionary activities, condemned to death, and taken to the place of execution; his sentence was commuted to imprisonment only after the ritual of execution had been carried up to the actual point of shooting. He genuinely thought he would die, and later that same day he wrote an extraordinary letter to his brother:

Brother, I'm not depressed and haven't lost spirit. Life everywhere is life, life is in ourselves and not in the external. . . . This idea has entered into my flesh and blood. Yes, it's true! That head which created, lived by the highest life of art, which acknowledged and had come to know the highest demands of the spirit, that head has been cut from my shoulders. . . . But my heart is left me, and the same flesh and blood which likewise can love and suffer and desire and remember, and this is, after all, life. *On voit le soleil!* (Mochulsky, 141).

His awakening had nothing to do with belief, and in his letter he thanks neither God nor the Tsar. He has simply realized what he did not know before. Life's fundamental goodness is now clear, and he wants his brother to know that through the years in prison this knowledge will be his strength. Using exactly the same details of the letter, Dostoevsky re-described his mock execution nearly twenty years later in *The Idiot*. The Prince is obsessed by two images of man-condemned: one is executed, the other pardoned. Myshkin's desire is to conduct his life in terms of what they, the condemned, know. So too with Father Zosimo, and finally Alyosha and Mitya, in *The Brothers Karamazov*. They know that "life is in ourselves and not in the external."

Survivors develop a faith in life which seems unwarranted to others. Dostoevsky did, and so did Bertrand Russell, to take a final example from *our* world. While in Peking during the winter of 1920-21, Russell came down with double pneumonia. Complications set in and "for a fortnight," as he tells us, "the doctors thought every evening that I should be dead before morning" (180). But with the coming of spring his health returned, and at some point during recovery Russell had an extraordinary experience, which he describes in Volume Two of the *Autobiography:*

Lying in my bed feeling that I was not going to die was surprisingly delightful. I had always imagined until then that I was fundamentally pessimistic and did not greatly value being alive. I discovered that in this I had been completely mistaken, and that life was infinitely sweet to me. Rain in Peking is rare, but during my convalescence there came heavy rains bringing the delicious smell of damp earth through the windows, and I used to think how dreadful it would have been to have never smelt that smell again. I had the same feeling about the light of the sun, and the sound of the wind. Just outside my windows were some very beautiful acacia trees, which came into blossom at the first moment when I was well enough to enjoy them. I have known ever since that at bottom I am glad to be alive (181-82).

That is the survivor's special grace. He or she is glad to be alive. For camp survivors this affirmation was seldom so joyous or easily won, and often it was made in stubborn bitterness. A survivor of the Nazi camp at Neubrandenberg speaks of having "no right to be unhappy." She goes on to stress the one solid insight which her experience gave birth to, a vision distilled from such masses of suffering as to bear the force of ethical imperative:

Be happy, you who live in fine apartments, in ugly houses or in hovels. Be happy, you who have your loved ones, and you also who sit alone and dream and can weep. Be happy, you who torture yourself over metaphysical problems, and . . . you the sick who are being cared for, and you who care for them, and be happy, oh, how happy, you who die a death as normal as life, in hospital beds or in your homes (Maurel, 140).

To talk like that a person must be very naive or very wise. Coming out of the concentration camps, such words reach the simplest of all knowledge—that life is

what counts, life whose internal destiny has had the
peace and the time to unfold. This is the wisdom of
Lear on the earth, stripped of everything but his pain,
who sees at last that ripeness is all.

Merely because they are survivors, the men and women
who passed through the camps are suspect in our eyes.
But when we consider the specific nature of their identity—not only as survivors, but survivors of *those* places
—suspicion deepens to shock and rejection. The concentration-camp experience represents an evil so appalling that we too, when we turn to face it, suffer psychic
unbalance. We too flounder in nightmare, in a torment
having nothing to do with us yet felt in some strange
way to be very much a part of our deepest, most secret
being. The terror of the camps is *with* us. Some hideous
impression of Auschwitz is in every mind, far removed
from conscious thought but *there;* and not only as a
repressed perception of historical events but as an image
which stirs up the demonic content of our own worst
fears and wishes. The image is with us; and anything
connected with it, anything which starts it into consciousness, brings with it a horror too large and intensely personal to confront safely. Thus A. Alvarez can say:

> The concentration camps are a dangerous topic to
> handle. They stir mud from the bottom, clouding
> the mind, rousing dormant self-destructiveness. In
> the last few years I personally have known half-a-
> dozen suicides or near suicides; and each has pref-
> aced his act with a fierce immersion in the liter-
> ature of the camps. That is why I suggested that
> these places, these crimes, have an existential

> meaning beyond politics or shock or pity. They
> have become symbols of our own inturned nihilism,
> which their disproportionately vast scale heightens,
> even justifies, by making individual suffering seem
> so insignificant (28).

He means that the dark, unspoken passion of fantasy
and desire, the whole of life's demonic undertow, has
found, at last, its specific image. The concentration
camps have given concrete form to the mind's most terrible enactments, such as before had been known
mainly from literature, from religion and folktale, from
dream and chthonic myth. The camps have justified and
made legitimate the imagination's fascination with destruction and pain and mutilation and defilement. By
"justified" I mean as history always justifies: not morally but in terms of priority in time, in the weight of real
over possible events, in irreversibility. Events, if they
are inclusive and compelling, provide imagination with
powerful occasions for mythical investment; and we
may at least speculate that for an unknown number of
years to come, the imaginative deployment of demonic
energy will use imagery drawn from the world of the
camps. The elegant perversity of de Sade, the demented
majesty of Dali and Lautréamont, seem timid and in-
dulgent compared with the forms now at our disposal
—imagery as old as the mind's infernal region but
which found its historical basis only after 1945.

The concentration camps are plainly an embodiment
of the archetype we call *Hell*. They were "hell on earth,"
as everybody says, and George Steiner has gone so far
as to suggest that they were a deliberate actualization of
the demonic tradition in art and literature and theology,
the most terrible instance of myth turning into history:

The camp embodies, often down to minutiae, the images and chronicles of Hell in European art and thought from the twelfth to the eighteenth centuries. It is these representations which gave to the deranged horrors of Belsen a kind of "expected logic." . . . The concentration and death camps of the twentieth century, wherever they exist, under whatever régime, are *Hell made immanent*. They are the transference of Hell from below the earth to its surface. They are the deliberate enactment of a long, precise imagining (53-54).

We must hope that Steiner is wrong, for if the kind of determinism implied in this "transference" is real—if man eventually and necessarily realizes his deep imaginings in fact—then the end will come, the bombs will fall, the myth of the World's End, imagined for millennia, will arrive in actuality. That is possible, but (employing Steiner's model) so is a new Golden Age, another of man's intenser imaginings. The mind of man holds everything, and our common fate may indeed, as Freud came to believe, be bound to the eventual outcome of a battle between conflicting psychic forces.

But finally I want to mark a lesser symmetry between Hell and the camps, simply the comparison itself. We make it all the time, and so do survivors. But for us it is misleading because the archetype informs our perception and we end up seeing the SS as satanic monsters and the prisoners as condemned souls. When we imagine what the survivor's experience must have been, we thus project our own fantasies, our own worst fears and wishes. From our remote vantage point only the horror is visible; the real behavior of survivors goes unobserved because it was covert, undramatic, not at all in accord with our expectations of heroism. And so it happens that we do not see them *as survivors*. They belong to that world, and in Hell there are none but the damned, none but the spiritually maimed unto death.

That mistake is easy to make. The typology of Hell was everywhere evident in the world of the camps. Steiner mentions such conventions as the "whips and hell-hounds," the "ovens and stinking air," the "mockery of the damned" (54). And yes, prisoners were mocked while whipped, they were torn to death by dogs, they breathed an air so utterly foul—and this is noted repeatedly by survivors—that nobody ever saw a bird fly over the camps. In its primitive Christian form, Hell is a place of darkness, thick with smoke and flame and stench, in which the damned are tormented by demons with pitchforks. What but Hell could this be?—

The burning had reached a peak that night. Every chimney was disgorging flames. Smoke burst from the holes and ditches, swirling, swaying and coiling above our heads. Sparks and cinders blinded us. Through the screened fence of the second crematory we could see figures with pitch forks moving against the background of flames. They were men from the special squad turning the corpses in the pits and pouring a special liquid so that they would burn better. A rancid smell of scorched flesh choked us. Big trucks passed us trailing a smell of corpses (Zywulska, 179).

That was Auschwitz in the fall of 1944, when the Jews of Hungary were being killed so fast and in such numbers that the usual gas-to-oven process had to be supplemented by pits in which the victims burned alive. "Yet from those flames," says Milton in *Paradise Lost,*

> No light, but rather darkness visible
> Serv'd only to discover sights of woe,
> Regions of sorrow, doleful shades, where peace
> And rest can never dwell, hope never comes
> That come to all. . . .

Milton's Hell is a "universe of death," and his high style should not deflect us from the fact that Auschwitz might be described in exactly the same terms (although not in Miltonic diction, which applied to the camps would generate lunatic irony). But the camps are there, in Milton's poem and in Dante's, in the under-realms of Homer and Virgil, in Shakespeare's *Lear*. From the world's literature we can abstract a set of conditions which make up the demonic or infernal depths as men have imagined them always. Northrop Frye has done this, arriving at an archetypal outline of the "world that desire totally rejects":

> . . . the world of the nightmare and the scapegoat, of bondage and pain and confusion. . . . the world also of perverted or wasted work, ruins and cata- combs, instruments of torture and monuments of folly (147).

Frye is describing an imaginary place, but he could be talking about a real world where men and women were forced to carry gigantic rocks back and forth to no purpose; where prisoners were hung by their hands on trees; where they lay face down in sewage and mud doing push-ups, and where to this day Dachau and Auschwitz stand as monuments to an age which is ours. The move from fiction to history argues the prophetic nature of art and perhaps even, as Steiner implies, a kind of cultural determinism. But it is also the special case of a more general relation between contrary realms of experience, between civilization and extremity, which can be formulated this way: what we experience symbolically, in spirit only, survivors must go through in spirit *and* in body. In extremity, states of mind become objective, metaphors tend to actualize, the word becomes flesh.

In *The Great War and Modern Memory,* Paul Fussell has noted the "curious literariness" of experience in the trenches. He observes that "one way of using canonical literature to help suggest the actuality of front-line experience was to literalize what before had been figurative" (165). Thus Shakespeare's metaphor for fallen majesty—Lear saying of his hand, "It smells of mortality"—becomes plain fact in the rank air of a world where corpses of men and horses lay rotting for months. Fussell concludes that "the drift of modern history domesticates the fantastic and normalizes the unspeakable" (74), and that beginning with World War I the perception of extreme events reveals a definite tendency: "The movement was toward myth, toward a revival of the cultic, the mystical, the sacrificial, the prophetic, the sacramental, and the universally significant. In short, toward fiction" (131).

But toward fiction which had actualized; and anyone sensitive to aesthetic form, sometimes called "significant form," is bound to wonder at this odd convergence of art and life. Describing a roundup of hundreds of women in the Soviet prison at Yaroslavl for transport to the camps, Eugenia Ginzburg remembers a small incident which, like a Joycean epiphany, revealed in a moment the shattering of personal life under Stalin.

"They made us give up the photographs of our children," she writes, and "I can still see the great pile of them on the stone floor of the yard" (268). That is already an example of significant form: the event in itself embodies and shows forth its larger meaning. But there is more, and Ginzburg goes on to remark:

> If, today, a film director were to show such a heap in close-up, he would certainly be accused of striving for a forced effect—especially if he were also to show a soldier's heavy boot trampling on the pile of cards, from which little girls in ribbons and boys in short pants looked up at their criminal mothers. The critics would say, "That's too much." Nevertheless, that is exactly what happened. One of the warders had to cross the yard and, rather than walk around the pile, stamped straight across the faces of our children. I saw his foot in close-up, as though it were in a film (268).

Extremity makes bad art because events are too obviously "symbolic." The structure of experience is so clear and complete that it appears to be deliberately contrived. But the great majority of books and documents by survivors are not consciously formal or deliberately shaped. Their testimony is in no way "literary," and yet everywhere great and terrible metaphors are embedded in events described. Hell first of all, and then "spiritual" states of being like purity and defilement, doom and salvation, death and rebirth. The following example involves a small massacre in a German forest:

> Then we were ordered to dig out the soil in the marked area. . . . others were told to break off small branches and twigs. . . . As evening closed in,

the S.S. men decided that the pit was deep enough.
. . . prisoners were told to stand in one row facing
the forest. . . . I watched the dancing rays of the
sun glinting through the trees. . . . Suddenly terrible
screams, accompanied by the crackle of rifle fire.
. . . There was a stampede to the right and to the
left. But the women could not run far. A few steps
and they were riddled with bullets. I stood in front
of the pit quaking. For a fleeting moment, through
glazed eyes, I saw my companions in the pit. Some
of them were still moving convulsively. I heard a
loud rifle volley, then silence and darkness. . . .
Is this death? . . . I try to raise my arm but can't.
I open my eyes but see nothing. . . . I am lying
inert in the dark. . . . I try to raise myself and I
find myself sitting up. Fresh branches are brushing
my head. It is dark and there are stars above me.
. . . As consciousness returns, my mind begins to
clear. . . . Trembling and weeping I cry out in a
faltering voice: "Are any of you alive? Come out if
you are!" And on the other side of the pit sits a
dark figure. "It's me," says Charlotte. But in the
pit itself no one moves. We two are the only survivors (Weiss, 74-75).

Bullets did not tear through her, her heart did not
stop. But she was certain—her body was certain—that
death was coming. She felt that she had died, she lay
for hours among the lifeless mass of her comrades, and
then got up. Is this the famous valley of death through
which souls pass? Is this resurrection? How much is
metaphor, how much plain fact? Or is there any longer
a difference? Archetypes have actualized in events so
exaggerated, so melodramatic and patently symbolic,

that no serious novelist, except perhaps in parody, would now attempt to treat them as art.

Man's interior drama, the height and depth of spiritual experience, has been writ large *in the world*. The concentration camps have done what art always does: they have brought us face to face with archetypes, they have invested body with mind and mind with body, they have given visible embodiment to man's spiritual universe, so that the primary states of good and evil are resident in the look and sound and smell of things. The essence of survival is passage through death; this way of speaking may be metaphorical for us, but not for survivors. Of course, a man or woman crawling out of a grave is not thinking of rebirth, may never have thought in such terms. For survivors of those ditches and pits there was only dumb pain. Still, they felt themselves die and then return to life, and the "objective correlative" of their ordeal was not a symbolic representation or a ritual entered imaginatively. It was the world itself, albeit a world such as we know through art and dream only. And here especially we must not be misled by our reliance on metaphor: the survivor is not a metaphor, not an emblem, but *an example*.

For us the camps are terminal images. They are the realized archetypes of eternal victimhood and of evil forever triumphant. As such they confirm most forcefully our vision of man as monster and victim. And yes, we are monsters. We are victims. But we are also survivors; and once we see the central fact about the survival experience—that these people passed *through* Hell—the archetypes of doom are, if not cancelled, at least less powerful in their authority over our perceptions. Survivors return from the grave, they come through Hell, and some, after descent into darkness and the defiling filth of underground sewers, rise again into the common world of sun and simple life. Existence at its boundary is intrinsically significant. Whatever we make of this fact, we should keep in mind that for survivors the struggle to live—merely surviving—is rooted in, and a manifestation of, the form-conferring potency of life itself.

RADICAL NAKEDNESS

Why, thou wert better in thy grave than to answer with thy uncovered body this extremity of the skies. . . . Unaccommodated man is no more but such a poor, bare, forked animal as thou art.

KING LEAR ON THE HEATH

ONE DIFFERENCE between Nazi and Soviet camps was that in the latter dying was a slower process. There was, though, this exception: during the early years of GULAG, when prisoners were sent into the arctic wastes to construct new slave sites, the ferocity of their ordeal was such, it took so many lives so fast, that later among Soviet inmates it became a sort of legendary standard by which to measure degrees of hardship in different camps. Dumped in the middle of nowhere, men and women had to answer the sky's extremity with, quite literally, nothing but themselves. Here is an "old" prisoner's story of those first days:

We found only unending forests and marshlands —areas upon which no human foot had ever trod before. For us nothing was prepared in advance. We were brought into the woods and told to build barracks and enclosures, to find water, to cut roads. . . . That was how the northern camps came into being. For months on end we slept in holes dug in the ground. We subsisted on a diet of dry rusks made of black bread and, in the summertime, on wild berries. We were unarmed in the struggle against a harsh nature. The biting cold, the strength-sapping labor, disease—these left alive

only a few of the original prisoners here. Even
among our guards the death rate was catastrophic.
. . . I can recall numerous cases of the "white
death"—when a prisoner simply remained alone in
the snow, not being able to muster the strength
to get up (Gliksman, 266).

That is an image of existence at its limit, the specific
case of the worst world possible. From it comes the
definition of extremity as a situation in which men and
women must live *without accommodation;* and to one
degree or another this was true of all the concentration
camps. All were places in which the human self was
stripped of spiritual as well as physical mediations, until
literally nothing was left to persist through pain and
time but the body itself.

To pass from civilization to extremity means to be
shorn of the elaborate system of relationships—to job,
class, tradition and family, to groups and institutions of
every kind—which for us provides perhaps ninety per-
cent of what we think we are. In the camps prisoners
lost their possessions, their social identity, the whole
of the cultural matrix which had previously sustained
them. They lost, in other words, the delicate web of
symbolic identifications available to men and women
in normal times. In Nazi camps they lost even their
names and their hair. They were reduced to immediate
physical existence through a process of de-sublimation
so abrupt and thorough that—in the plainest, starkest
sense—nothing remained of what the self had been:

You lost the capability of proving to yourself, in a
moment of doubt, that you are still the same human being you were when you came here. That
being is gone, and only a miserably wretched crea-

ture remains in her place. A naked creature deprived of everything and avidly covering her body with someone else's sweat-saturated garments in spite of keen disgust (Szmaglewska, 78).

Or as Viktor Frankl discovered after his first hours in Auschwitz:

While we were waiting for the shower, our nakedness was brought home to us: we really had nothing now except our bare bodies—even minus hair; all we possessed, literally, was our naked existence (13).

In Soviet camps, new prisoners were regularly robbed of vital possessions, especially warm clothing, by the ubiquitous gangs of *urkas* (criminals). In Nazi camps the reduction to nakedness involved a specialized set of procedures. But in either case the outcome was total loss, and the survival struggle therefore began with a search for minimal items of accommodation, clothing or a blanket or the indispensable cup or bowl. Very often —since new prisoners had not yet learned to "organize" —the things they needed could only be got by trading bread. And once inmates did find some essential item, they had to carry it on their own bodies as the only sure protection against theft: "The picture of a Soviet camp inmate in his torn quilted outfit is incomplete without a rough, rusty tin cup fastened to his belt and dangling at his side" (Gliksman, 239). Survivors did the same in German camps, and even then nothing was secure. At random moments camp officials conducted searches for "illegal" possessions, and anything not hidden was liable to be confiscated:

They would rush at us, slapping, striking, shouting, emptying our bags, feeling the hems of our dresses and opening them to remove the paper windbreakers, confiscating the mittens and even the belts—those precious pieces of string. They found everything, they stripped us of everything and took it all away, crying sabotage. And we started off again from scratch (Maurel, 16-17).

Starting "from scratch" is in fact the survivor's permanent condition. He or she is always on the line, always being pushed back again and yet again to the outmost edge of existence. In the Nazi camps, a typical method of "thinning out" sick and exhausted prisoners was to force thousands of them to stand undressed for hours in winter weather. Then the survivor's nakedness was radical indeed, nor could he escape the terrible conclusion that in extremity everything depends on the body. All about him stood that "poor, bare, forked animal" which is, as old Lear said, "the thing itself." None of us would wish to depend on something so puny, so frail and easily harmed as the human body. But for survivors there is nothing else.

In civilized circumstances, life unfolds in accord with a fate largely inward, and as it does, the past grows in reality and significance. The growth of a time which is *our* time, the process of chance becoming destiny through an irreversible chain of events, gives us much of the uniqueness we feel about ourselves as individuals. The self comes to feel grounded in its personal past, as indeed it is; and the more our lives are burdened by distress and uncertainty, the more we value what has already been lived. We cling to the past, sometimes in

pride, more often in guilt and confusion, but cling all
the same. And increasingly as we age we turn in memory to our particular past as to a world in reserve for
rest and assurance. Novelists know this especially well.
What they seek through their work is a reclamation of
the past which will proclaim the reality of human selfhood to its deepest foundations.

But again survivors are different. Their immediate
past is collective rather than personal, a past identical
for everyone who came through the common catastrophe. Memory and selfhood are rooted, often traumat-
ically, in events which define the individual not as an
individual but as a participant in, and the embodiment
of, decisive historical experience. Alain Resnais made
this point with great tenderness in *Hiroshima Mon
Amour,* a film in which the struggle of the lovers to
know one another reaches resolution only when each
understands and admits that she *is* Nevers, he *is* Hiroshima. No purely private destiny can match their historical fate, no personal agony can equal the war's massive pain. A past of this kind is the basis of the survivor's
identity *as* a survivor, and becomes manifest in the act
of bearing witness.

In another sense, however, survivors have no past at
all—not, that is, while actually going through the camp
experience. They have been uprooted from their former
life, stripped of connection with it, and forced, finally,
to adjust their sense of reality to conditions drastically
different from those of that other world. Not even
memories remain—partly because fear and pain concentrate awareness on the present, but mainly because survivors cannot *risk* remembering. As a Soviet survivor
says: "The experienced Russian camp inmates kept
advising us to forget—for our own sakes—our past
lives. Otherwise, they maintained, homesickness would

soon undermine our resistance" (Gliksman, 278).
Which is to say that as long as life depends on ruthless
suppression of despair and self-pity, survivors cannot
afford to remember. They cannot drift in and out of
the past as we do; not often, in any case, and never for
longer than a moment's passing weakness. Those who
begin to "live in the past," as we say, inevitably lose
their hold on the present. They become less attentive,
less disciplined, and in the end they die. To remain
strong, therefore, the survivor must cultivate a kind of
strategic oblivion:

> From this point of view the perfect prisoner does
> not exist, but there are men who, after several
> years behind barbed wire, can control their mem-
> ories far better than their primitive instincts; a
> relentless discipline of oblivion has erected an
> impassable barrier between their past and their
> present (Herling, 98).

The process of being stripped bare culminates when the
past and present are torn apart, as if some actual rending, some intimate severance of the self from prior roots,
has occurred:

> There were still naive prisoners among us who
> asked, to the amusement of the more seasoned
> ones who were there as helpers, if they could keep
> a wedding ring, a medal or a good-luck piece. No
> one could yet grasp the fact that everything would
> be taken away.
>
> I tried to take one of the old prisoners into my
> confidence. Approaching him furtively, I pointed to
> the roll of paper in the inner pocket of my coat and
> said, "Look, this is the manuscript of a scientific

book. I know what you will say; that I should be grateful to escape with my life, that that should be all I can expect of fate. But I cannot help myself. I must keep this manuscript at all costs; it contains my life's work. Do you understand that?"

Yes, he was beginning to understand. A grin spread slowly over his face, first piteous, then more amused, mocking, insulting, until he bellowed one word at me in answer to my question, a word that was ever present in the vocabulary of the camp inmates: "Shit!" At that moment I saw the plain truth and did what marked the culminating point of my psychological reaction: I struck out my whole former life (Frankl, 12).

But if the past was struck out, what of time still to come? What of the future with the sense of possibility it gives us, the feeling of life unfolding toward fulfillment which supports so much of personal identity and which, in troubled times, nourishes the will to push on? But of course, in the concentration camps there was no future. At very best, tomorrow meant more of the same. Death might be seconds away, and each day was an agony so endless as never to be got through. Under such circumstances, thinking of the future was even more painful than remembering the past:

A day begins like every day, so long as not to allow us reasonably to conceive its end, so much cold, so much hunger, so much exhaustion separates us from it: so that it is better to concentrate one's attention and desires on the block of grey bread, which is small but which will certainly be ours in an hour, and which for five minutes, until we have devoured it, will form everything that the law of the place allows us to possess (Levi, 57).

That is a constant theme of survivors: to concentrate on this day, this five minutes, this small need or pleasure. They endure from one day to the next, from one hour to another, "on a short-term basis," as one survivor says —which meant, for example, "eating what one was given without laying aside for the future, since no future was certain" (Berkowitz, 126).

As the war neared its end, prisoners in the German camps were aware of the coming liberation. They also knew that general massacres were scheduled (some of which took place); and once the death marches began, deliverance seemed remote indeed. Some part of the will to live *was* rooted in the hope of ultimate release, however unlikely that possibility might seem at any particular time. Many survivors must surely have drawn upon this faint last hope to carry them through those final days. But almost always this kind of hope was covert, like a repressed desire which affects behavior although it remains unconscious. For Soviet prisoners, the chance of release was even more improbable. Too many inmates, on the day their term was up, were sentenced to another ten or twenty years. At the end of the war, rumors of amnesty were widespread; but here too, the best protection against despair was not to hope:

Such exaltation was usually followed by deep depression when the imagined zero hour had passed without incident. If, after such a swing from hope to despair, we did not wish to suffer mental instability . . . we had to develop our own technique for preserving our sense of balance. Many became thorough pessimists because of this (Gollwitzer, 81).

To live by looking ahead, as we do, was not possible in the camps. One Soviet prisoner, after serving his sentence of 3,650 days, was told that instead of release his term had been prolonged "indefinitely." That same day he died, for no visible reason. As one of his surviving comrades said, "I can only guess what was happening in his heart, but one thing is certain—that besides despair, pain, and helpless anger, he felt also regret for his thoughtless faith in hope" (Herling, 33). The chances for survival and freedom were so logically improbable that no hope, as we know hope, could be allowed into consciousness. The despair thus generated would be too much to bear. How, standing through the hours of winter roll-call in Auschwitz, could anyone be said to hope or believe in a future?

It is as if this present moment of existence in camp with the thousands of motionless figures were frozen like the plants at the bottom of a lake, whose surface is covered by a thick layer of ice. And neither your longing eyes nor the efforts of your young arms nor your warmest thoughts can pierce that heavy layer of ice which spreads over your life. No fist, no matter how strong, can crack this barrier with its blow (Szmaglewska, 110).

The temptation to despair was thus compounded by the temptation to hope, in a situation where both were deadly. And as might be expected, April was indeed the cruellest month. The desire to remember, to have one's past self born again, was worst in the spring. The return of growth and fruitfulness, the whole of life's

promise implicit in a blade of new grass, suggested a
future that in the survivor's case was mockery. In extremity life proceeds by rejecting hope, by refusing to
consider the future:

> If you lack the strength to resist the call of the earth
> awakened by spring . . . [you] had better grab up
> a spade, a wheelbarrow, do any task within the
> camp and glue your eyes on the faded barracks.
> Not for one moment let yourself forget that you are
> in a concentration camp. You will be much less
> unhappy if you do not experience the dreams, and
> then face the rude awakenings. . . . In order not to
> become insane from the wonder of life pulsating all
> around you in newly awakening nature . . . it is
> better to bury yourself in the camp, as a rock is
> embedded and cannot move from its place (Szma-
> glewska, 170).

Prisoners in the camps did struggle, did resist, did
plan and carry through revolts. But not, again, with
hope as we know it. Sanity depended on always expect-
ing the worst, on the realism of doomed men and women
still holding out. This, finally, is the attitude survivors
take: they might make it, they probably won't, but they
will not stop trying.

Past and future mean little to men and women dying,
for whom reality resides in a scrap of string or bread.
If survivors thought of things elsewhere, they did it
wistfully or with a moment's fierce desire, but without
prolonged belief. Everything about the camp experience
conspired to reduce them to where they were and what
they were—living bodies in a place of death. Gone were

the myths and institutions, the symbols and technologies which in normal times allow the self to transcend and lose sight of its actual situation. An apt image of civilization, crude as this may sound, is that of a man sitting on a toilet reading a book. He is there, of course, but in consciousness he is elsewhere. The physical act he performs, and the biological identity it confirms, are neither visible nor in any sense significant. But for men and women in extremity this same event, minus the book, the privacy and the comfort of a clean toilet bowl, becomes an activity requiring tense attention. Survivors are reduced to primal acts and to an awareness circumscribed by primitive needs. They are naked to the roots, radically compressed to their essence as creatures of flesh.

When in ordinary circumstances we discuss the question of basic needs, the most fundamental of all, the need to excrete, is of course never mentioned. There will always, however, be much talk of two others, which for most of us represent man's "animal" side. Hunger and sex, we say, are ineradicable needs; and with hunger there is no doubt. But with sex the case is less clear, despite the belief that sex is as fundamental as hunger. It isn't. One of the striking things about the concentration-camp experience—and there is enormous evidence on this point—is that under conditions of privation and horror the need for sex disappears. It simply is not there, neither in feeling nor in fantasy, neither the desire nor the drive. As one survivor says, "Many of us young men ceased to have any sexual feelings whatever; Karel and I, during all the time we were in Treblinka, and for long afterwards, were men in name only" (Sereny, 237). Or as another puts it, "After two or three weeks of the regime at Maidanek, sex problems disappeared. Women lost their periods; men lost their urge" (Donat, 183). In Buchenwald, according to the report of a doctor imprisoned there, "one hundred per cent of the female prisoners ceased to menstruate at the very beginning of their term of captivity; the function did not reappear until months after their liberation" (Weinstock, 235). And another survivor, this time from Auschwitz, observes that "even in his dreams the prisoner did not seem to concern himself with sex" (Frankl, 31).

The same thing occurred in Soviet camps. As one survivor says: "Oh, how we made fun of ourselves! Someone said that it was a miracle of nature that we had to urinate, . . . otherwise we would forget we had a sex organ" (Gilboa, 236). Another humorous remark, which in time became a camp proverb, was a standard answer to new prisoners when they asked if survival was possible: "Oh, yes, but you won't want to sin with women" (Grossman, 321). The loss of sexual will was a universal phenomenon in the camp world, despite the fact that erotic activity was present in limited degree, more in Soviet than in German camps. And as the following statement suggests, whether or not one was capable of sexual functions depended very much on the degree of hunger, exhaustion and distance from danger:

One thing I noticed throughout my experience in these camps for men and women was that sex was not the pervading problem one might have expected. There were always a number of liaisons. Guards and other officials kept a few chosen girls well fed . . . but in general, in the camps I knew, human vitality was at such a low ebb that lust found little place (Fittkau, 204).

There was more sexual activity in the Soviet camps because there was more opportunity; but also because conditions were less openly horrible. In any of the camps, however, sex was possible mainly for special prisoners. *Kapos* and cooks, for example—men and women safer and better fed—took advantage of their positions and indulged themselves, often recklessly. Gangs of *urkas* in the Soviet camps were a constant danger to any woman alone; and women in Soviet camps often tried to become pregnant, because bearing a child earned the mother six months of freedom from heavy labor assignments. But still, such instances were not typical. In places like Buchenwald and Auschwitz the SS set up brothels in an attempt to dissipate the growing strength of the political underground. They assumed —incorrectly, it turned out—that powerful prisoners would enjoy themselves at the expense of their comrades. Only criminals went, men in league with the SS and untroubled by the need for solidarity.

The fact would seem to be that when men and women are exhausted and starving, sex is not important, and that it likewise tends to be absent when the threat of death becomes constant. A momentary brush with death may very well intensify sexual desire, but when dread becomes prolonged and seeps to the core of one's being, the capacity for erotic fulfillment is ruined. Perhaps too, disappearance of sexual desire in the camps was a biological phenomenon in service of collective survival. For if a state of nature had prevailed, men and women fighting among themselves for sexual privilege, the kind of community which grew up among prisoners would have been more difficult and open to betrayal. And it would seem, finally, that the most powerful depressors of sexual need are horror and moral disgust. The stationmaster at Treblinka, who directed incoming trains (but who was also a secret agent in the Polish underground), reports that once the killing started, he and his wife could no longer make love: "Of course there was no question of a normal sexual life; we felt we lived in a cemetery; how could one feel joy there?" (Sereny, 155). Sexual joy is one of life's chief blessings, and the biological drive which enforces it is very strong. Even so, eros begins to govern human behavior only after a critical level of safety and well-being has been attained. If this runs counter to Freud's view—that civilized rather than primitive conditions repress erotic need—so be it. Behavior which does not support day-to-day existence tends to vanish in extremity. We may fairly conclude that what remains is indispensable.

Survivors act as they do because they have to; and what their predicament reveals is that in extremity life and humanness depend on the same set of activities. This amounts to saying that when external props collapse, survivors fall back on life itself. A survivor of Treblinka speaks for all those like himself when he says:

> I have read more or less everything that has been written about this subject. But somehow no one appears to have understood: it wasn't *ruthlessness* that enabled an individual to survive—it was an intangible quality, not particular to educated or sophisticated individuals. Anyone might have it. It is perhaps best described as an overriding thirst—perhaps, too, a *talent* for life, and a faith in life (Sereny, 183).

He is referring to something which enables men and women to act spontaneously and correctly during times

of protracted stress and danger. There is no evidence—
nor should the above statement be construed—to suggest that this capacity is exclusive to a particular class,
race, culture or nation. The survivor just quoted is
describing how it felt to him *as experienced;* and for
the phrase "talent for life" we might substitute "magic
will" or "imperishable power" or "life itself" or any of
the other phrases survivors use. The reference is always
to something other and greater than the personal ego, a
reservoir of strength and resource which in extremity
becomes active and is felt as the deeper foundation of
selfhood. This is as much as survivors can say of their
experience, but in coming to this limit we touch upon a
further implication—a view reached precisely at the
limit of personal experience. Survivors act as if they
were *prepared* for extremity; as if anterior to learning
and acculturation there were a deeper knowledge, an
elder wisdom, a substratum of vital information biologically instilled and biologically effective.

We may at least speculate that through long periods
of extremity, survival depends on life literally—life,
that is, as the biologists see it, not as a state or condition
but as a set of activities evolved through time in successful response to crisis, the sole purpose of which is to
keep going. Life continues, defends itself, expands. It
does this by answering environmental challenges with
countless behavioral patterns designed to deal with dis-
turbance and threat. Behavior which proves successful
for any particular species *over the long run* enters its
genotype and becomes "innate." To be sure, this happens
by chance, with many failures, and through unimagin-
ably long ages of time. From phylum to phylum, furthermore, the elements of such patterns differ greatly, but
each will possess some fixed response to danger, some

settled way of meeting major needs, including those of defense and repair. Survival, in this case, depends on a basic fund of "biological wisdom," to use C. H. Waddington's phrase, with which all living creatures are endowed. Stripped of everything but life, what can the survivor fall back upon except some biologically determined "talent" long suppressed by cultural deformation, a bank of knowledge embedded in the body's cells. The key to survival behavior may thus lie in the priority of biological being—which is to say that the properties of life itself may best account for the rather surprising fact that under dehumanizing pressure men and women tend to preserve themselves in ways recognizably human.

To suggest that the survivor's behavior is biologically determined is to assume a number of principles which, from the perspective of the biological sciences, can be considered "facts of life." The first is that almost all behavior in the individual as in the society directly or indirectly serves the general cause of survival. The second is that any particular pattern of behavior is the outcome of millions of years of trial-and-error experience which, once it has crystallized, passes from generation to generation through genetic transmission. The third, which follows from the first two, is that primary forms of behavior are innate, the ingrained inheritance of all life-experience in a particular line of descent. The fourth is that these facts apply as much to man as to other life-forms. The whole of this view is summed up in two broad statements by J. Z. Young: "the capacity to continue is precisely the central characteristic of life" (108); and "the characteristics of human life are the activities by which human continuity is maintained" (8).

There is no question of "vitalism" here, no transcendental life-force or *élan vital* in Bergson's sense. And there is no question of "teleology" either, no grand design, no pre-established harmony tuning up at our expense as Teilhard de Chardin, for example, would have liked us to think. Life has no purpose beyond itself; or rather, having arisen by chance in an alien universe, life is its own ground and purpose, and the entire aim of its vast activity is to establish stable systems and endure. There is nothing especially mysterious about this, although the *feeling* of life—existence experienced subjectively—bears mystical significance and power. Life goes forward through the collision of populations with environments; how fast or slow this happens depends on the interaction of genetic potential and natural selection, "the outcome," as E. O. Wilson puts it, "of the genetic response of populations to ecological pressure" (32).

For any particular life-form, this much is certain: it is what it is, and behaves as it does, as the result of the whole of its past. "Every living being is *also* a fossil," says Jacques Monod:

> Within it, all the way down to the microscopic structure of its proteins, it bears the traces if not the stigmata of its ancestry. This is yet truer of man than of any other animal species by dint of the dual evolution—physical and ideational—that he is heir to (160).

Man's immediate past goes back two million years. The line of hominid descent goes back fifteen to twenty million years. And in the deepest sense, man's inheritance goes back to the appearance of life on earth, some two billion years ago; time enough to acquire the ground-sense necessary to survive in proven ways. And whether we call the configuration of man's biologically determined behavior his "biogram," as Earl W. Count has suggested, or his "biological infrastructure," as Lionel Tiger argues, the basic point is clear: survival behavior reveals a fixed system of activity, biological in origin, which is specific to humanness as such.

It would be strange indeed, with so many millions of years of survival-experience packed into our genes, if at some deep involuntary level we did not possess capacities specially geared to cope with extreme situations. In the beginning there was nothing but extremity, nothing but the random rush of life in a touch-and-go struggle against extinction. Against the constant threat of oblivion, tendencies had to be developed which would increase the capacity to continue. The process of evolution is thus a perpetual gathering of information, on levels ever more complex, which works to preserve existence not only under normal conditions (which means conditions already adjusted to), but especially in time of disaster. Part of the uniqueness of man is that in addition to normal adaptation, he seems adjusted to *possible* dangers, to threat as a potential condition. At least in its essentials, human behavior may be understood as "a repertoire of possible reactions" (Young, 604) to a range of possible events. The particular response will depend on the situation being faced.

The survivor's experience therefore calls us back to something which Enlightenment rationalism, with its hope of starting over, spent two centuries denying: what N. Tinbergen calls "the innate foundations of behaviour" (6). The biologist's assumption is that like any other animal, man possesses "instinctive" forms of basic behavior. Such deep-seated tendencies are constantly transformed by an endless and often chaotic variety of cultural modes, but they exist all the same, and operate most decisively when life is threatened. What separates man from all other life-forms is of course civilization, although in *Animal Architecture* von Frisch suggests that even in this respect we are not entirely special. Animals also build worlds, modify environments, transform instincts and situations. But they never attain freedom as we know it, never move as we do beyond the immediate dangers and restrictions of physical existence. "Yet, for all his cultural achievements," as S. E. Luria reminds us, "man does not escape biological evolution; he only modifies its effects on himself" (145). Through technical and symbolic means our biological fate has been transcended and denied. But for all that, we are still bodies, and our inescapable condition is that of any other life-form. Each quantum of behavior is another leaf on the barely visible branches of a tree whose trunk never shows as long as civilization works efficiently, but which comes starkly into view as soon as, by some terrible mischance, the leaves and branches fall.

Students of biology are generally agreed that a human "biogram" exists. But one aspect of man's biological make-up—the capacity to modify perceptions and behavior through culture—makes the rest of the biogram difficult to identify. It is there, the sure foundation of everything else. But like any foundation, it lies belowground and is easy to miss as we marvel at the building it supports. Human behavior, at least in normal times, is always a mix of instinct and learning, of immediate and mediated response; and this distinction, as E. O.

Wilson points out, is crucial to further understanding of man as a biological creature:

> One of the key questions, never far from the thinking of anthropologists and biologists who pursue real theory, is to what extent the biogram represents an adaptation to modern cultural life and to what extent it is a phylogenetic vestige. Our civilizations were jerrybuilt around the biogram. How have they been influenced by it? Conversely, how much flexibility is there in the biogram, and in which parameters particularly? Experience with other animals indicates that when organs are hypertrophied, phylogeny is hard to reconstruct. This is the crux of the problem of the evolutionary analysis of human behavior (548).

The problem with man is that his evolution involved a series of "quantum jumps" which radically transformed the use and quality of inherited traits. The relation of human behavior to its own phylogenetic past and to that of other species is therefore unclear. But on one point biologists agree: man is the culmination of a tendency toward social organization which appears everywhere in the biosphere. Certainly there were societies before there were men. The cell itself is a kind of social organization, and any two-cell animal is in fact two animals who long ago worked out a system of mutual support. Primates likewise solved the problem of survival, millions of years before the appearance of man, by evolving social orders which include systems of communication and hierarchy, of mating and care for the young, of food-gathering, territory and defense. The typical primate social group, as Hans Kummer observes, is "an ever-present tool of survival" (36). Man could not have emerged without these prior achievements, and thus Konrad Lorenz argues:

> If it were not for a rich endowment of social instincts, man could never have risen above the animal world. All specifically human faculties, the power of speech, cultural tradition, moral responsibility, could have evolved only in a being which, before the very dawn of conceptual thinking, lived in well-organized communities (246).

Precisely how this occurred is not known; but that human society did emerge from earlier societal forms, and that man is social *by nature,* are aspects of the human condition beyond doubt. I stress this point because thinkers as influential as Rousseau and Freud have insisted that man is anti-social, and that society is held together more by force and fear than by any innate disposition on the part of its members. Precisely this view underlies the mistaken notion that a "state of nature" prevailed in the concentration camps, or that a war of all against all necessarily erupts as soon as constraints are removed. Far otherwise, primary aspects of the camp experience—group formation, "organizing," sharing and the giving of gifts—are evidence amounting to proof that in man social instincts operate with the authority and momentum of life itself, and never more forcefully than when survival is the issue. In *The Social Life of Animals,* W. C. Allee has observed that even among organisms like bacteria and spermatozoa there are signs of "communal activity"; these tiny creatures live more successful *en masse,* and Allee concludes that "a sort of unconscious co-operation or automatic mutualism extends far down among the simpler plants and

animals" (88). Animals—men and women included—
tend to survive better in groups, and not only in terms
of help and defense, but just by being near each other.
One survivor of the Nazi camps describes her struggle
in these terms: "As soon as one is alone one thinks:
What's the use? Why do it? Why not give up? . . . With
others, one keeps going" (Delbo, 116).

To cite striking similarities between animal and human behavior, as ethologists like Lorenz and Tinbergen
have done; or to extrapolate a human "biogrammar"
from the activities of primates, as Lionel Tiger and
Robin Fox have proposed, is not to prove that human
existence is governed by biological "laws." From the
evidence at hand, however, we may at least speculate
on the close relation of basic human acts to similar
kinds of behavior in other life-forms. A possible conclusion is that behavior specific to man exists within a
continuum of life-activities so fundamental and essential
to existence that, in one form or another, they may be
found throughout the biological realm. Bernhard
Rensch's *Biophilosophy* does indeed approach such
conclusions; and although few biologists would care to
back him up, the tendency is more and more to expect
a "new synthesis," beyond the recent wedding of Dar-
win and genetics, which might arrive finally at a unified
theory of life including man and culture.

Wilson points out that "the rate of change in a particular set of cultural behaviors reflects the rate of
change in the environmental features to which the behaviors are keyed" (560). This means that with the
fall from civilization into extremity, with that fierce descent to nakedness, significant changes should have
appeared in the behavior of survivors—*if,* that is, the
basic components of humanness are culturally determined and culturally upheld. But apart from the period

of initial collapse, no dramatic change took place. The elementary forms of social being remained active, dignity and care did not disappear. These facts argue an agency stronger than will or conscious decision, stronger even than the kind of practical intelligence which made the need for moral order and collective action obvious. Something innate—let us think of it as a sort of biological gyroscope—keeps men and women steady in their humanness despite inhuman pressure.

The depth and durability of man's social nature may be gauged by the fact that conditions in the concentration camps were designed to turn prisoners against each other; but that in a multitude of ways, men and women persisted in social acts. Fear and privation increased irritability but did not keep inmates from joining in common cause. In fact protracted death-threat is the condition which brings social instincts to their strongest pitch. This is true of animals as well. Group formation in defense against predation is common from insects to primates, and protective strategies often depend on intricate systems of communication and mutual aid. Among many species of birds and other vertebrates, furthermore, the degree of social cohesion is proportionate to the degree of food scarcity or other negative features of the environment. The more pressure from without, the more "solidarity" from within. For animals as for man, return to community is an inborn reaction to danger and prolonged stress. Only under highly favorable conditions can a society tolerate anti-social forms of behavior. We can pretend we owe nothing to anyone, but survivors know they need each other.

Integral to survival at the social level—again in man as in other species—is some form of warning technique, and this is almost certainly the basis of the survivor's obsessive need to "tell the world." The will to bear witness, as we have seen, is an involuntary reaction to extreme situations. Survivors do not so much decide to remember and record, as simply find themselves doing it, guided by the feeling that it *must* be done. Earlier I suggested that this act can be compared to a scream, but perhaps it *is* a scream—a special version of the social animal's call to its group—and thus a signal of warning and appeal which on the human level becomes the process of establishing a record and thereby transmitting information vital for both moral and practical reasons. We learn what to fear, what to call evil and therefore what to call good, by absorbing the costly experience of others. It seems possible that a real connection, biologically encouraged, exists between the survivor's act of witness and the kind of primate behavior described by Washburn and Hamburg in the following instance:

> In the Nairobi Park there are many groups of baboons that are accustomed to cars. A parasitologist shot two of these baboons from a car and eight months later it was still impossible to approach the group in a car. It is most unlikely that even a majority of the animals saw what happened and the behavior of the group was based on the fear of a few individuals. *It is highly adaptive for animals to learn what to fear without having to experience events directly themselves* (DeVore, 619).

Our strongest instinctive reactions tend to be those provoked by fear and threat, and often the response is most intense—and this may account for the frenzy of political struggle—when the danger is collective. While indirectly of benefit to individuals, behavior concerned with warning and rescue—the whole complex of action surrounding the scream—is geared primarily to survival at the level of the group. "With the alarm call," as Robert Ardrey puts it, "the perception of the first becomes the property of the group"; and this kind of behavior is so widespread that "the alarm signal, in almost all species, becomes the very criterion for society itself" (73-74). E. O. Wilson states that "warning calls seem prima facie to be altruistic" (123), at least insofar as to sight the danger is to be exposed to it, which likewise argues the individual's instinctive concern for the safety of the larger group. Insofar as these facts bear on human behavior, we can appreciate the sense of urgency so apparent when survivors bear witness. For a Jew in Auschwitz, the annihilation of his or her people was *possible;* and in an even broader respect—since not only Jews bear witness—the survivor's scream arises from the deepest fear of all, that mankind, or indeed all life, is now endangered.

Much of the behavior of survivors may thus be traced to the "biosocial" roots of human existence; and not their behavior merely, but also the extraordinary stubbornness of will which characterizes action in extremity—the furious energy of a will impersonal and stronger than hope, which in an accurate, unmetaphorical sense can only be that of life itself. But survivors do more than maintain moral sanity and establish bonds among themselves. They also struggle to preserve dignity as something which cannot be dispensed with. This too may be the specifically human enactment of a biological imperative. I say *human* here, because we do not know if anything like a sense of dignity exists for other life-forms. Robinson Jeffers wrote poem after poem celebrating what he called the dignity of lone animals, the puma, the hawk, the wild boar, saying that only animals possess dignity because only they are at all times in complete accord with their essential nature and cannot be corrupted from it. That is exactly the condition survivors struggle to preserve, but with a difference. Animals remain true to their essence because they are not free to betray themselves. Only man has a choice, and only man, furthermore, has a kind of consciousness which transforms the condition of dignity into a sense and a feeling. And here man may truly stand alone. Dignity in its human context presupposes self-awareness and a deliberate resistance to determination by external forces. In this way, as Erving Goffman suggests in *Asylums,* dignity becomes an essential element of selfhood:

> The practice of reserving something of oneself from the clutches of an institution is very visible in mental hospitals and prisons but can be found in more benign and less totalistic institutions, too. I want to argue that this recalcitrance is not an incidental mechanism of defense but rather an essential constituent of the self (319).

"Recalcitrance" splendidly describes survivors in their stubborn refusal to be completely shaped by their environment. In the camps, dignity was equated with selfhood because it was the only thing left, the one dimension of intimate existence beyond the enemy's reach. As one survivor says: "We had no longer homes to defend. All we had was our human dignity, which was our home, our pride, our only possession—and the moral strength to defend it with" (Perl, 60). Stripped of everything, prisoners maintained moral identity by holding some inward space of self untouchable, and they did it by the way in which the body itself was carried and cared for. The need for dignity and the will to resist are closely related. They may in fact be identical: two ways of warding off capitulation, of saying No, of insisting upon the observance of a boundary between self and world.

Survivors make radical adjustments in order to live; but at the same time, and also in order to live, they strive to keep themselves *fundamentally* unchanged by the pressures to which they respond. In this they are like life itself, which is flexible and conservative at the same time, which is polymorphic in the extreme and yet which exhibits a definite development of greater and greater order, accompanied by a tendency toward irreversibility, on both the individual and the species levels. Life is unlike all other phenomena because it defies entropy. While everything else in the universe is "running down," life is "running up." In some sense this is true of the human self also. It too defies entropy and resists dispersal; it too spends much energy and anguish keeping itself tightly whole—a kind of moral effort we ordinarily refer to as "maintaining integrity"—and works to adjust without losing the continuity of its basic organization. The comparison I am making is pure speculation, of course; it could hardly be otherwise. And yet how apt, in the survivor's case, to take seriously the idea that mankind is life conscious of itself; as if basic biological processes, transformed by consciousness, do indeed reappear as activities specific to selfhood.

Human beings need and desire to be part of a larger whole, to join with their fellows and even, in moments of great passion, to lose the sense of self entirely. That is the basis of sex and religion, of politics and society.

But just as much, men and women yearn for solitude, they struggle fiercely for an existence apart, for an integrity absolutely unbreachable. That is the basis of dignity, of personality, of the egoism which fuels creation and discovery, and finally of the sense of individual "rights." But throughout the whole of the biosphere a similar duality is evident. From polymers to man, life-forms are perpetually merging, joining, establishing symbiotic and societal modes of relation for mutual benefit. At the same time, however, particular life-forms are differentiating themselves from others, individuation becomes more and more pronounced, a species diverges within itself (even as others converge) until successful breeding no longer occurs. Strangest of all is the tendency of individual organisms to reject tissue from any other organism not "recognized" as "self." This phenomenon, commonly referred to as "immuno-rejection," suggests a tendency toward radical selfhood at the very basis of life. On the human level, this activity of keeping whole and inviolate, this constant resistance to the penetration of otherness, is the essence of dignity. And its organic parallel is striking. "Our theme," say J. Z. Young, "is that living things act as they do because they are so organized as to take actions that prevent their dissolution into the surroundings" (12).

What separates man from the rest of the living world, his blessing and his curse, is consciousness. At a fairly recent stage in the evolutionary past, man reached awareness not only of things around him, but of himself and his condition. Once this occurred, characteristics like dignity and conscience could develop, the process of civilization could begin in earnest, because now, for the first time, an animal had become capable of altering its fate. With self-consciousness came the ability to prepare and manipulate, to make changes in basic conditions, and finally to transform or reject the biological foundations of existence. "Biological evolution transcended itself when it gave rise to man," says Theodosius Dobzhansky; and by "transcend" he means "to go beyond the limits of, or to surpass the ordinary, accustomed, previously utilized or well-trodden possibilities of a system" (44-45). Transcendence in exactly this sense is the achievement on which the whole of civilization rests; and we know approximately how and when this process began by two items of anthropological evidence: tools and ritual burial.

Primates use tools—they work food and sometimes defend themselves with rocks and pieces of wood—but no animal except man systematically *makes* tools. As Bernard Campbell says in *Human Evolution:* "An ape cannot conceive the tool without seeing it. He cannot see the stick in the plank or a hand-axe within a piece of rock. This man alone can do" (335). To do that is a sure sign of imagination and forethought, of purpose understood, and of a willingness to tolerate delay in order to proceed with greater efficiency. There is plenty of evidence that at some stage in the pre-dawn of human experience—perhaps two million years in the past—men became aware of themselves sufficiently to start working upon their material condition. The tool is the beginning of technology, a process which, once in motion, becomes as inevitable in its development as evolution itself.

But the rise to self-consciousness was decisive for an even more important reason. When men and women became conscious of themselves they became aware of death and of their own vulnerability. And they began to notice, as no other animal can, the frightfulness of in-

finite spaces opening everywhere around them. As Dobzhansky observes, "death-awareness is a bitter fruit of
man's having risen to the level of consciousness" (69).
What began a billion years earlier as neurological response to environmental stimuli, with man came to
climax in terror. And with it came the need for spiritual
defense and preservation: the need for a technology of
the emerging soul, for symbols, rituals, myths—all the
vehicles of transformation through which death and
nothingness vanish and reappear as "higher" life and
meaning. Culture and death are profoundly related; and
again—this time in René Dubos's words—we have
evidence:

> At least a hundred thousand years ago, Neanderthal
> man buried his dead with offerings in a crouched
> position oriented from east to west, and in some
> cases on beds of wildflowers. Some form of ulti-
> mate concern may thus be coeval with mankind.
> The need to symbolize death and the afterlife may
> constitute one of the attributes that set man com-
> pletely apart from the animal kingdom (60-61).

Ritual burial is the oldest form of collective symbolic
activity, and the fact that the dead were almost always
painted with red ocher—a practice reserved for ritualized
and sacred objects—implies some rude degree of religious consciousness. We know with fair certainty, moreover, that religion and sacred rites were a central part
of the oldest civilizations (those whose artifacts and
records still exist); and what these developments imply
is that culture—the symbolic machinery of transcendence—began with death-dread. It began, that is, with
the will to negate the biological dimension of human
existence.

Man as man came into being when the evolution of consciousness forced upon him the knowledge of his own condition. This was simultaneously the birth of civilization—of technology and culture—and from then onward, more and more rapidly, man has been shaped and guided by culture at least as much as by the dictates of physical need. Civilization has long surpassed the immediacy of the survival situation (for those at the top, that is); its ancient roots are hidden, deliberately obscured. The function of technology is to serve physical and economic needs well enough for us to ignore them. The function of culture is to negate the primal facts of nothingness and death. Both aspects of civilization reduce consciousness of our condition as biological creatures. And in the end both breed contempt for life.

The split between mind and body, between man's "higher" and "lower" natures, is not only a consequence but the major goal of this process. The spirit soars, preens, consoles itself in a freedom gained by repressing consciousness of the body and its needs. A short-hand formula for the whole of this endeavor would be (keeping Freud in mind): where body was, there shall spirit be. Western civilization is the negation of biological reality; and unavoidably, since life and death are inextricable, the denial of death comes finally to be a denial of life. At its worst it results in overt hostility to life, as if only by killing, only by administering death with style and majesty, could death itself be mastered. In *Death in the Afternoon,* Hemingway speaks of "the feeling of rebellion against death which comes from its administering":

Once you accept the rule of death thou shalt not kill is an easily and a naturally obeyed commandment. But when a man is still in rebellion against death he has pleasure in taking to himself one of the Godlike attributes; that of giving it. This is one of the most profound feelings in those men who enjoy killing (233).

Our possible fate is that man's last act will indeed be Godlike. He will lift his finger and destroy all life on earth and thereby—literally—kill death. Already we have machines to make the "final solution" truly final. Just this predicament has given rise to the survivor as a significant human type. Survivors are those who have escaped the murderous circle of our retreat from death, men and women shoved violently back upon a biological wisdom long unheeded. The survivor is the figure of all those who, in Hemingway's words, have had to "accept the rule of death," and for whom "thou shalt not kill" has become a "commandment" *naturally* obeyed. There is terrible irony in this, for whereas awareness of death generates firm care for life, death-denial ends in a fury of destruction. Perhaps the ultimate difference between civilization and extremity—between *us* and *them*—is captured in a single stark comment by Octavio Paz: "Facing death the spirit is life, and facing the latter, death" (52).

The survivor is the man or woman who has passed through the "crisis of civilization" we talk about so much. That some kind of crisis is brewing—that civilization no longer works well even for the few—is evident. The man-made death of one hundred million people in little more than fifty years is proof enough. At the heart of our problems is that nihilism which was all along the destiny of Western culture: a nihilism either unacknowledged even as the bombs fall or else, as with Hitler or Stalin, demonically proclaimed as the new salvation. And it was inevitable; for when mythic structures collapse and symbolism fails, the choice is ourselves or nothing. Nietzsche was the great prophet of this development, and he foresaw the choice we would face. "What is dawning," he wrote in 1886, "is the opposition of the world we revere and the world we live and are. So we can abolish either our reverence or ourselves" (45). So far we have preferred to abolish ourselves, and how easy it has been. Amid high cant and pieties obscenely cynical, whole cities and peoples are wiped out. The value of life has been reduced to zero, to excrement.

This cannot go on for much longer, and the fact that now the whole of life is threatened may be—with luck—a turning point. "As with all evolution's creations," says S. E. Luria, man's "biological fate is to make do, to survive as a species by the skin of his teeth" (120). It seems that for all our achievements and dreams we have not, after all, defeated the body's crude claims. And this, again, is the survivor's special importance. He is the first of civilized men to live beyond the compulsions of culture; beyond a fear of death which can only be assuaged by insisting that life itself is worthless. The survivor is evidence that men and women are now strong enough, mature enough, awake enough, to face death without mediation, and therefore to embrace life without reserve.

Whenever we hear of this or that atrocity, and especially when the revelations of terrorism and modern warfare upset our faith in civilization, we speak with knowing bitterness about the "thin veneer" of culture and about how swiftly man's "real" nature reveals itself under stress. Part of our torment is that we think we know what lies beneath the surface. We look into the darkness of our own hearts and behold every kind of destructiveness—the whole demonic surge of savagery erupting daily in war, torture, genocide, or spilling out imaginatively in so much of modern art and literature. What we have not seen is that our rage stems from nihilism, and that nihilism is the outcome of allegiance to a mind-body split which makes hateful the body and its functions, and storms in spiteful execration against the whole of existence as soon as life is no longer justified by firm belief in "higher" values. And we have altogether missed the fact that beyond our lust for disaster there is another, far deeper stratum of the human psyche, one that is life-affirming and life-sustaining.

A biological wisdom exists, prompting us to know that in life's own needs the spirit can find a home. Not noble or god-approved, not especially dramatic or sublime as in the old days, but rooted in the plain happiness of work and communion with others, and in the small shared universe of physical joy which is our due as creatures of flesh. And also this; that in birth and growth and fruitfulness there is meaning enough to quiet our hunger for high cause—concrete significance, perpetually renewed in the striving and sorrow and brief accomplishment which living demands from day to day. The sun is here, as survivors and condemned men know. Life, the earth in its silence, is all there is. How infinitely sad that Hegel's "secularization of the spirit" reached its first fulfillment in the concentration camps.

Man's kinship with the gods is over. Our Promethean moment was a moment only, and in the wreckage of its aftermath a world far humbler, far less grand and self-assured, begins to emerge. Civilization will either destroy itself, and us with it, or alter its present mode of functioning. And culture—that "life of the mind" as we call it—will of course continue but likewise change. The realm of ideas and symbols will have to be lived closer to the bone, real unmetaphorical bone, bone frail as grass and easily crushed. And as for an ethic based on selfless love, that dream cost two thousand years of misery, and like "faith in humanity" came to its end in Auschwitz, in Hiroshima, in the forests of Vorkuta. What remains to us now is simple care, a care biologically inspired and made active through mutual need.

One thinks of the statues of Classical Greece, the Periclean perfection of their grace and poise, their integral strength meant to symbolize the spirit of man. One thinks of the great painting and sculpture of the Renaissance, the incredible beauty of that faith in a humanness "larger than life." And one thinks now of the survivor, not as an emblem or a symbol, but as he is, in rags and dirt, his face the face of anyone, his eyes just barely bright. His soul lives *in* his flesh, and what his body says is that the human spirit can sink this low, can bear this torment, can suffer defilement and fear and unspeakable hardship and still exist. In our time the fate of man and the fate of life are one, and we would be less than wise to ignore the survivor's voice. Not only his scream, and the horror that provoked it, but his voice in simple talk to others like himself. To new prisoners on their first night in Sachsenhausen, a survivor spoke these words:

I have not told you of our experiences to harrow you, but to strengthen you. . . . Now you may decide if you are justified in despairing.

BIBLIOGRAPHY

The bibliography is in two parts. The first, Original Testimony, contains the direct testimony of actual survivors. The second part, Secondary Sources, contains all other references. The amount of literature by survivors, or in which survivors are quoted, is truly vast, and only a very small part of it is listed below. No adequate bibliography exists. For an introduction to testimony by survivors in English and English translation, see Janet Ziegler, *World War II: Books in English, 1945-65* (Stanford, Calif.: Hoover Institute, 1971), Section VI, "Social Impact of the War." For a list of bibliographies on the literature of the Jewish catastrophe, see Jacob Robinson and Philip Friedman, *Guide to Jewish History under Nazi Impact* (New York: YIVO Institute for Jewish Research, 1960), Chapter Sixteen, "Collections of Personal Narratives and Anthologies." Survivors of the concentration camps have left records in more than twenty languages, most not in English.

Page references in the text are from the first edition listed.

I ORIGINAL TESTIMONY

Akhmatova, Anna. *Selected Poems,* tr. Richard McKane (London: Oxford University, 1969).

Berg, Mary. *Warsaw Ghetto: A Diary,* tr. Norbert and Sylvia Glass (New York: L. B. Fisher, 1945).

Berkowitz, Sarah Bick. *Where Are My Brothers?* (New York: Helios, 1965).

Bernard, Jean-Jacques. *The Camp of Slow Death,* tr. Edward Owen Marsh (London: Victor Gollancz, 1945).

Bettelheim, Bruno. "Individual and Mass Behavior in Extreme Situations," *Journal of Abnormal and Social Psychology,* Volume 38, No. 4, October 1943, pp. 417-52.

————. *The Informed Heart* (Glencoe, Ill.: Free Press, 1960; London: Thames & Hudson, 1961).

Birenbaum, Halina. *Hope Is the Last To Die,* tr. David Welsh (New York: Twayne, 1971).

Buber-Neumann, Margarete. *Under Two Dictators,* tr. Edward Fitzgerald (New York: Dodd, Mead; London: Victor Gollancz, 1949).

Ciszek, Walter J. *With God in Russia* (New York: McGraw-Hill, 1964).

Cohen, Elie A. *Human Behavior in the Concentration Camp,* tr. M. H. Braaksma (New York: Norton, 1953; London: Jonathan Cape, 1954).

Delbo, Charlotte. *None of Us Will Return,* tr. John Githens (New York: Grove, 1968).

Donat, Alexander. *The Holocaust Kingdom* (New York: Holt, Rinehart and Winston, 1965; London: Corgi, 1967).

Ekart, Antoni. *Vanished Without Trace,* tr. Egerton Sykes and E. S. Virpsha (London: Max Parrish, 1954).

Fittkau, Gerhard A. *My Thirty-Third Year* (New York: Farrar, Straus, 1958).

Frankl, Viktor E. *From Death-Camp to Existentialism,* tr. Ilse Lasch (Boston: Beacon, 1959).

Friedman, Philip. *Martyrs and Fighters* (London: Routledge & Kegan Paul, 1954).

Gilboa, Yehoshua A. *Confess! Confess!,* tr. Dov Ben Aba (Boston: Little, Brown, 1968).

Ginzburg, Eugenia Semyonovna. *Journey into the Whirlwind,* tr. Paul Stevenson and Max Hayward (New York: Harcourt, Brace & World, 1967; London: Collins, 1970).

Glatstein, Jacob; Knox, Israel; and Margoshes, Samuel. *Anthology of Holocaust Literature* (New York: Atheneum, 1973).

Gliksman, Jerzy. *Tell the West* (New York: Gresham, 1948).

Gluck, Gemma La Guardia. *My Story* (New York: McKay, 1961).

Goldstein, Bernard. *The Stars Bear Witness,* tr. Leonard Shatzkin (New York: Viking, 1949; London: Victor Gollancz, 1950).

Gollwitzer, Helmut. *Unwilling Journey: A Diary from Russia,* tr. E. M. Delacour (Philadelphia: Muhlenberg; London: SCM Press, 1953).

Grossman, Moshe. *In the Enchanted Land,* tr. I. M. Lask (Tel-Aviv: Rachel, 1960-61).

Hardman, Leslie H. *The Survivors: The Story of the Belsen Remnant* (London: Vallentine, Mitchell, 1958).

Hart, Kitty. *I Am Alive* (London and New York: Abelard-Schuman, 1962).

Heimler, Eugene. *Night of the Mist,* tr. André Ungar (New York: Vanguard; London: Bodley Head, 1959).

Herling, Gustav. *A World Apart,* tr. Joseph Marek (New York: Roy; London: Heinemann, 1951).

Kantor, Alfred. *The Book of Alfred Kantor* (New York: McGraw-Hill, 1971).

Kaplan, Chaim A. *The Warsaw Diary of Chaim A. Kaplan,* tr. Abraham I. Katsh (New York: Collier, 1973). Under the title *Scroll of Agony* (New York: Macmillan, 1965; London: Hamish Hamilton, 1966).

Kessel, Sim. *Hanged at Auschwitz,* tr. Melville and Delight Wallace (New York: Stein & Day, 1972; London: Talmy Franklin, 1973).

Klein, Gerda Weissman. *All But My Life* (New York: Hill & Wang, 1957; London: Elek, 1958).

Knapp, Stefan. *The Square Sun* (London: Museum Press, 1956).

Kogon, Eugen. *The Theory and Practice of Hell,* tr. Heinz Norden (New York: Farrar, Straus, 1953; London: Secker & Warburg, 1950).

Kraus, Ota, and Kulka, Erich. *The Death Factory: Document on Auschwitz,* tr. Stephen Jolly (Oxford: Pergamon, 1966).

Kuznetsov, A. *Babi Yar,* tr. David Floyd (New York: Farrar, Straus & Giroux, 1970; London: MacGibbon & Kee, 1967).

Lengyel, Olga. *Five Chimneys: The Story of Auschwitz,* tr. Paul P. Weiss (Chicago: Ziff-Davis, 1947; London: Mayflower, 1972).

Levi, Primo. *The Reawakening*, tr. Stuart Woolf (Boston: Little, Brown, 1965). Under the title *The Truce* (London: Bodley Head, 1965).

————. *Survival in Auschwitz*, tr. Stuart Woolf (New York: Collier, 1969). Under the title *If This Man Is a Man* (New York: Orion, 1959; London: Orion, 1960).

Lewinska, Pelagia. *Twenty Months at Auschwitz*, tr. Albert Teichner (New York: Lyle Stuart, 1968).

Lingens-Reiner, Ella. *Prisoners of Fear* (London: Victor Gollancz, 1948).

Lipper, Elinor. *Eleven Years in Soviet Prison Camps*, tr. Richard and Clara Winston (London: World Affairs, 1951; Hollis & Carter, 1952).

London, Artur. *The Confession*, tr. Alastair Hamilton (New York: Ballantine, 1971). Under the title *On Trial* (London: Macdonald, 1970).

Mandelstam, Nadezhda. *Hope Against Hope*, tr. Max Hayward (New York: Atheneum, 1970; London: Harvill, 1971).

Maurel, Micheline. *An Ordinary Camp*, tr. Margaret S. Summers (New York: Simon & Schuster, 1958). Under the title *Ravensbruck* (London: Blond, 1958).

Newman, Judith Sternberg. *In the Hell of Auschwitz* (New York: Exposition, 1964).

Nork, Karl. *Hell in Siberia*, tr. E. Brockett (London: Robert Hale, 1957).

Nyiszli, Miklos. *Auschwitz: A Doctor's Eyewitness Account*, tr. Tibere Kremer and Richard Seaver, with "Foreword" by Bruno Bettelheim (New York: Frederick Fell, 1960; London: Panther, 1967).

Pawlowicz, Sala. *I Will Survive* (New York: Norton; London: Muller).

Perl, Gisella. *I Was a Doctor in Auschwitz* (New York: International Universities Press, 1948).

Poller, Walter. *Medical Block, Buchenwald* (London: Souvenir, 1961).

Rappaport, Ernest A. "Beyond Traumatic Neurosis," *International Journal of Psycho-Analysis*, XLIX, Part 4, 1968, pp. 719-31.

————. "Survivor Guilt," *Midstream*, XVII, August-September 1971, pp. 41-47.

Ringelblum, Emmanuel. *Notes from the Warsaw Ghetto*, tr. Jacob Sloan (New York: McGraw-Hill, 1958).

Roeder, Bernhard, *Katorga,* tr. L. Kochan (London: William Heinemann, 1958).

Rousset, David. *The Other Kingdom,* tr. Ramon Guthrie (New York: Reynal and Hitchcock, 1947).

Semprun, Jorge. *The Long Voyage,* tr. Richard Seaver (New York: Grove; London: Weidenfeld & Nicolson, 1964).

Sereny, Gitta. *Into That Darkness* (New York: McGraw-Hill, 1974; London: Deutsch, 1974).

Solomon, Michael. *Magadan* (New York: Auerbach, 1971).

Solzhenitsyn, Alexander. *One Day in the Life of Ivan Denisovich,* tr. Ralph Parker (New York: Dutton; London: Pall Mall, 1963).

————. *The First Circle,* tr. Thomas P. Whitney (New York: Harper & Row; London: Collins, 1968).

————. *The Cancer Ward,* tr. Rebecca Frank (New York: Dial, 1968; London: Bodley Head, 1968-69).

Szalet, Leon. *Experiment "E,"* tr. Catherine Bland Williams (New York: Didier, 1945).

Szmaglewska, Seweryna. *Smoke over Birkenau,* tr. Jadwiga Rynas (New York: Henry Holt, 1947).

Thorne, Leon. *Out of the Ashes* (New York: Rosebern, 1961).

Unsdorfer, S. B. *The Yellow Star* (New York and London: Thomas Yoseloff, 1961).

Vrba, Rudolf. *I Cannot Forgive* (New York: Grove; London: Sidgwick & Jackson, 1964).

Wdowinski, David. *And We Are Not Saved* (New York: Philosophical Library, 1963; London: W. H. Allen, 1964).

Weinstock, Eugene. *Beyond the Last Path,* tr. Clara Ryan (New York: Boni and Gaer, 1947).

Weiss, Reska. *Journey Through Hell* (London: Vallentine, Mitchell, 1961).

Weissberg, Alexander. *The Accused,* tr. Edward Fitzgerald (New York: Simon & Schuster, 1951). Under the title *Conspiracy of Silence* (London: Hamish Hamilton, 1952).

Wells, Leon W. *The Janowska Road* (New York: Macmillan, 1963; London: Jonathan Cape, 1966).

Wiechert, Ernst. *Forest of the Dead,* tr. Ursula Stechow (New York: Greenberg, 1947).

Wiesel, Elie. *Night,* tr. Stella Rodway (New York: Avon, 1969; London: Fontana, 1973).

————. *A Beggar in Jerusalem,* tr. Lily Edelman and Elie Wiesel (London: Weidenfeld and Nicolson, 1970).

————. *One Generation After,* tr. Lily Edelman and Elie Wiesel (New York: Avon, 1972; London: Weidenfeld & Nicolson, 1971).

————. *The Oath,* tr. Marion Wiesel (New York: Random House, 1973).

Wigmans, Johan H. *Ten Years in Russia and Siberia,* tr. Arnout de Waal (London: Darton, Longman and Todd, 1964).

Zywulska, Krystyna. *I Came Back,* tr. Krystyna Cenkalska (London: Dennis Dobson, 1951).

II SECONDARY SOURCES

Allee, W. C. *The Social Life of Animals* (New York: W. W. Norton, 1938; London: Heinemann, 1929).

Alvarez, A. *Beyond All This Fiddle* (New York: Random House, 1969; London: Allen Lane, 1968).

Ardrey, Robert. *The Social Contract* (New York: Atheneum; London: Collins, 1970).

Arendt, Hannah. *Eichmann in Jerusalem* (New York: Viking; London: Faber & Faber, 1963).

Bluhm, Hilde O. "How Did They Survive?" *American Journal for Psychotherapy,* Volume II, No. I, 1948, pp. 3-32.

Braudel, Fernand. *Capitalism and Material Life 1400-1800,* tr. Miriam Kochan (New York: Harper & Row, 1974).

Campbell, Bernard G. *Human Evolution* (Chicago: Aldine, 1974; London: Heinemann Educational, 1967).

Camus, Albert. *The Plague,* tr. Stuart Gilbert (New York: Random House; London: Hamish Hamilton, 1948).

Count, Earl W. "The Biological Basis of Human Sociality," in *Culture,* ed. M. F. Ashley Montagu (New York: Oxford University, 1968).

DeVore, Irven, ed. *Primate Behavior* (New York and London: Holt, Rinehart and Winston, 1965).

Dobzhansky, Theodosius. *The Biology of Ultimate Concern* (New York: World, 1967; London: Rapp & Whiting, 1969).

Douglas, Mary. *Natural Symbols* (London: Barrie and Jenkins, 1973).

Dubos, René. *A God Within* (New York: Scribner's, 1972; London: Angus & Robertson, 1973).

Elkins, Stanley M. *Slavery* (Chicago: University of Chicago, 1959; 2d ed., Chicago and London: University of Chicago, 1969).

Frisch, Karl von. *Animal Architecture*, tr. Lisbeth Gombrich (New York: Harcourt Brace Jovanovich, 1974).

Frye, Northrop. *Anatomy of Criticism* (Princeton: Princeton University, 1957).

Fussell, Paul. *The Great War and Modern Memory* (New York and London: Oxford University, 1975).

Goffman, Erving. *The Presentation of Self in Everyday Life* (Garden City: Doubleday, Anchor Books 1959; London: Allen Lane, 1969).

———. *Asylums* (Chicago: Aldine, 1962; London: Penguin, 1970).

Hemingway, Ernest. *Death in the Afternoon* (New York: Scribner's, 1960; London: Penguin, 1971).

Hobbes, Thomas. *Leviathan* (New York: Bobbs-Merrill, 1958; London: Dent Everyman's, 1973).

Hoppe, Klaus D. "The Psychodynamics of Concentration Camp Victims," *The Psychoanalytic Forum*, Volume I, No. I, 1966, pp. 76-85.

Housepian, Marjorie. "The Unremembered Genocide," *Commentary*, XLII, September 1966, pp. 55-61.

Jaspers, Karl. *The Question of German Guilt*, tr. E. B. Ashton (New York: Dial, 1947).

Kummer, Hans. *Primate Societies* (Chicago: Aldine, 1971).

Lifton, Robert Jay. *Death in Life: Survivors of Hiroshima* (New York: Random House, 1967; London: Weidenfeld & Nicolson, 1968).

———. *History and Human Survival* (New York: Random House, 1970).

———. "Questions of Guilt," *Partisan Review*, XXXIX, Winter 1972, pp. 514-30.

Longinus. "On the Sublime," in *Criticism: The Major Texts*, ed. Walter Jackson Bate (New York: Harcourt Brace Jovanovich, 1970).

Lorenz, Konrad. *On Aggression*, tr. Marjorie Keer Wilson (New York: Harcourt, Brace & World; London: Methuen, 1966).

Luria, S. E. *Life: The Unfinished Experiment* (New York: Scribner's, 1973).

Malamud, Bernard. *The Fixer* (New York: Farrar, Straus & Giroux, 1966; London: Eyre & Spottiswoode, 1967).

Mao Tse-Tung. *Selected Military Writings of Mao Tse-Tung* (Peking: Foreign Languages, 1967).

Mauss, Marcel. *The Gift: Forms and Functions of Exchange in Archaic Societies,* tr. Ian Cunnison (London: Cohen & West, 1954; Routledge, 1969).

Mochulsky, Konstantin. *Dostoevsky: His Life and Work,* tr. Michael A. Minihan (Princeton: Princeton University, 1971).

Monod, Jacques. *Chance and Necessity,* tr. Austryn Wainhouse (New York: Knopf, 1971; London: Collins, 1972).

Moore, Barrington, Jr. *Reflections on the Causes of Human Misery* (Boston: Beacon; London: Allen Lane, 1972).

Nietzsche, Friedrich. *The Will to Power,* tr. Walter Kaufmann and R. J. Hollingdale (New York: Random House, 1967; London: Weidenfeld & Nicolson, 1968).

Paz, Octavio. *Claude Lévi-Strauss: An Introduction,* tr. J. S. Bernstein (Ithaca, N.Y.: Cornell University, 1970; London: Jonathan Cape, 1972).

Portmann, Adolf. *Animals as Social Beings* (New York: Viking; London: Hutchinson, 1961).

Rensch, Bernhard. *Biophilosophy,* tr. C. A. M. Sym (New York: Columbia University, 1971).

Ricœur, Paul. *The Symbolism of Evil,* tr. Emerson Buchanan (New York: Harper & Row, 1967).

Russell, Bertrand. *The Autobiography of Bertrand Russell 1914-1944* (New York: Bantam, 1969; London: Allen & Unwin, 1967-71).

Schopenhauer, Arthur. *On the Basis of Morality,* tr. E. F. J. Payne (New York: Bobbs-Merrill, 1965).

Skinner, B. F. *Beyond Freedom and Dignity* (New York: Knopf, 1971; London: Jonathan Cape, 1972).

Steiner, George. *In Bluebeard's Castle* (New Haven: Yale University; London: Faber & Faber, 1971).

Tiger, Lionel. *Men in Groups* (New York: Random House, 1969; London: Nelson, 1970).

Tiger, Lionel, and Fox, Robin. *The Imperial Animal* (New York: Holt, Rinehart and Winston, 1971; London: Secker & Warburg, 1972).

Tinbergen, N. *The Study of Instinct* (Oxford: Clarendon, 1951).

Waddington, C. H. *The Ethical Animal* (London: Allen & Unwin, 1960).

Wilson, E. O. *Sociobiology: The New Synthesis* (Cambridge: Harvard University, 1975).

Young, J. Z. *An Introduction to the Study of Man* (Oxford: Oxford University, 1971).